MOVE IT!

STUDENTS' BOOK

T0385800

SPLIT EDITION

4B

KATHERINE STANNETT AND FIONA BEDDALL

SERIES CONSULTANT: CARA NORRIS-RAMIREZ

Reading and Listening	Speaking and Pronunciation	Writing
Work Experience Jobs of the Future? 🔈 An ideal summer job 🔈 Dictation	Phone language **Pronunciation:** /ɚ/ and /ɔr/	An email about plans **Writing File:** Expressing degrees of certainty
Life in a Seaside Town Shipwrecks, Pirates and a Sunken Treasure! 🔈 A tour guide talking about the *Cutty Sark* 🔈 Dictation	Asking for and giving directions **Pronunciation:** Weak vs strong form of *was*	A field trip report **Writing File:** Planning a field trip report
Explorers: Where Next? Next Stop: Mars 🔈 Building colonies in the future 🔈 Dictation	Giving warnings **Pronunciation:** Elided syllables	An application letter **Writing File:** Letter writing
I'm Right Behind You Who's Watching You? 🔈 Talking about CCTV cameras 🔈 Dictation	Explaining and apologizing **Pronunciation:** /ɛr/, /i/ and /eɪ/	An opinion essay **Writing File:** Expressing opinions
Prom Night Coming of Age 🔈 Coming-of-age traditions 🔈 Dictation	Reaching an agreement **Pronunciation:** /ʃ/, /ʒ/ and /dʒ/	A problem page **Writing File:** Referencing

(5) Work for It

Vocabulary • Work collocations

1 Match the items in the picture (1–11) to these words. One word is missing from the picture. Then listen, check and repeat.
2.14

appointments
copies
email
front desk
inquiry
meeting
office supplies
payments
phone
presentation *1*
report
spreadsheet

MEETING ROOM

SALES REPORT
JANUARY - APRIL

2 Choose the correct options.

1 attend *a meeting / a spreadsheet*
2 answer *an appointment / the phone*
3 deal *at the front desk / with inquiries*
4 write *a meeting / a report*
5 give *inquiries / a presentation*
6 make *an appointment / a phone*
7 check *emails / a meeting*
8 work *some copies / at the front desk*
9 prepare *a spreadsheet / at the front desk*
10 take *an appointment / payments*
11 make *some copies / a meeting*
12 order *office supplies / inquiries*

2.15, 2.16 **Pronunciation Unit 5** page 67

3 Listen to Dan and Julie. What did they do
2.17 yesterday? Use the collocations from Exercise 2.

Dan worked at the front desk; …
Julie …

4 Work in pairs. What do you think these people do at work? Use the words in Exercise 2 to help you.

- a secretary
- a teacher
- a police officer
- a salesperson
- a mechanic

Brain Trainer Unit 5
Activities 1 and 2
Go to page 62

Reading

1 Read the webpage quickly. Choose the best description.

1 It describes different job opportunities for young people when they leave school.
2 It advises students on how to apply for a job.
3 It describes a way to get work experience before leaving school.

2 Read the webpage again. Are the statements true (T), false (F) or don't know (DK)?

2.18

1 Alleghany High School students do a semester of work experience. *T*
2 Rema is still in school.
3 Jed didn't like the people at the building supplies company.
4 Babblefish wants to be a math teacher.
5 Clarkson is good at repairing vehicles.
6 Clarkson isn't looking forward to going out on a test drive.
7 Batgirl is going to help with teaching sports on her placement.
8 She probably won't use the phone during her week at the gym.

3 What about you? Ask and answer.

1 Have you done any part-time jobs or had any work experience?
2 What kind of work would be interesting/useful as work experience for you?

Jed

Work Experience

← → C ⌂

Rema

Today we're looking at work experience. Juniors and seniors at Alleghany High School in Virginia can do a semester of work experience. It's a great chance to find out about the skills you will need for the world of work.

Rema did her work experience at a local cell phone store and loved it! When she left school, she applied for a job there, and now she's the area manager.

Jed got a work placement with a building supplies company. He prepared some spreadsheets for the sales team, attended a marketing meeting and made a lot of copies. "Some of the work was boring," said Jed, "but the people were great."

COMMENTS

Tell us about your plans. What are you going to do for your work experience?

I'm going to spend a week at an elementary school because I want to be a teacher. I'm going to observe some math classes and accompany the children on a field trip to a farm. I'll probably be very tired by the end of the week, but I'm really looking forward to it. BABBLEFISH

I have a placement with the Police Vehicle Workshop, where mechanics repair police cars. I love trying to understand how vehicles and machines work, so I think this placement will be really interesting. I'm going to help the mechanics, wash and clean the cars and, best of all, I'm going to go out on some test drives with the mechanics! CLARKSON

I love sports, especially tennis, so I got a work placement at my local gym. I'm going to assist with beginners' tennis coaching and organize the sports equipment. I'll probably also work at the front desk, make appointments for gym training sessions, take payments and deal with telephone inquiries. BATGIRL

Grammar • Will/Going to

will
Are you thirsty? I'll get you a drink. I'll probably be very tired by the end of the week.

going to
I'm going to spend a week at an elementary school. The chair is broken. You're going to fall!

Grammar reference page 118

1 Study the grammar table. Match the beginnings (1–2) to the endings (a–d) of the sentences to complete the rules.

1 We use *will*
2 We use *going to*

a to make predictions about the future.
b to talk about plans and intentions.
c to express sudden decisions.
d to make a prediction when we have some evidence.

> **Watch Out!**
> We use these time phrases to talk about the future:
> Next week/month/year
> In three days
> By Tuesday/the weekend/the end of the month
> In the next week/month/year

2 Match the statements and questions (1–6) to the sentences (a–f).

1 I started my new job today. *d*
2 What are your vacation plans?
3 We missed the bus.
4 We don't have any bread.
5 Do you want to watch a DVD at my house?
6 I'm sorry, I can't meet you later.

a I'll go to the store and get some.
b That's a great idea. I'll bring some popcorn.
c We're going to be late.
d I think I'll really enjoy it.
e I'm going to visit my grandmother in the hospital.
f We're going to visit San Francisco.

3 Choose the correct options, *will* or *going to*.

1 Next year I'*ll* / '*m going to* study physics.
2 You're driving too fast! Look at the car in front of you! You'*ll* / '*re going to* crash!
3 **A** Do you want a ham or a cheese sandwich?
  B I'*ll* / '*m going to* have a cheese sandwich.
4 I think you'*ll* / '*re going to* be a millionaire before you're 25.
5 *Is your brother going to* / *Will your brother* play in the baseball game tomorrow?

4 Complete the conversation with the correct form of the verbs.

A Hi, Ben. I just put the kettle on. Do you want tea or coffee?
B Thanks, Mom. I ¹ *'ll have* (have) a coffee, please.
A ² .... (you/see) Uncle Joe this afternoon?
B No, I ³ .... (be). I ⁴ .... (play) tennis with Jen. Why?
A Oh, I want to return this book to him.
B Well, I ⁵ .... (take) it to his house after tennis.
A Are you sure about tennis? Look at the clouds! It ⁶ .... . (rain)
B You're right. Jen ⁷ .... (probably/cancel) the game. I ⁸ .... (call) her now.

5 Work in pairs. Write two true statements and two false statements about your weekend plans. Can your partner guess the false statements?

A I'm going to play tennis with my cousin.
B True!
A Yes. I'm going to bake a chocolate cake.
B False!
A No, it's true.

Vocabulary • Job qualities

1 Look at these words and phrases. Check the
2.19 meanings in a dictionary. Then listen and repeat.

accurate	analytical	excellent IT skills
experienced	good communicator	leadership qualities
organized	~~patient~~	practical
punctual	reliable	team player

Word list page 27
Workbook page 128

2 Complete the sentences with the words from
Exercise 1.

1 A *patient* person stays calm and is prepared
to wait if necessary.
2 An .... person is efficient and is good at
planning his/her time.
3 A .... can express himself/herself well and can
give information in a clear way.
4 A .... person is never late.
5 A person with .... is good at being the most
important person in a group and likes
making decisions.
6 An .... person looks at information carefully
and finds the important facts and figures.
7 A .... person likes doing active, useful work.
8 A .... works well with other people and thinks
about all the people in his/her group.
9 An .... person has already done a similar job.
10 A .... person is someone you can trust
and believe.
11 A person with .... is good at using computers.
12 An .... person is very careful with his/her work
and hardly ever makes mistakes.

3 Work in pairs. Use words and phrases from
Exercise 1 to complete the job advertisements.

Editorial Manager

We are looking for a person with [1] *leadership
qualities* to be the manager of a team of six.
The ideal candidate will be [2] .... and has worked
in publishing for at least five years. We need a [3] ....
who can give clear and interesting presentations
to large groups of people.

Veterinary Assistant

Our large, friendly Vet's Surgery is
looking for a [4] .... person who can help
our vets with everyday work. It's
important to be [5] .... , as we open at
8:30 every morning, and our ideal
candidate will also have [6] .... and can
update our spreadsheets.

School Receptionist

We are looking for a [7] .... person
who can stay calm and won't
panic in our busy office. We
want an [8] .... person who can
plan meetings and keep our
reports and files in order. Our
ideal School Receptionist will be
a [9] .... who can work together
with a large group of teachers
and school administrators.

Data Analyst

Our statistics department
has a vacancy for an [10] ....
worker to look at health
data and collect statistics.
We need [11] .... information,
with no mistakes. The Data
Analyst works with important
and confidential information,
and we want a [12] .... person
for the job.

4 What about you? In pairs, ask and answer.

1 Tell your partner about a time in your life when
you achieved something or did something
really well.
2 Which qualities does this achievement show?

**Brain Trainer Unit 5
Activity 3**
Go to page 62

Speaking and Listening

1 Look at the photo. What is Archie doing? Does Holly look interested or bored?

2 Read and listen to the conversation.
2.20 Check your answers.

3 Listen and read again. Answer the questions.
2.20
1 What does Holly ask Archie to look for?
a job in the paper
2 What is the name of the store?
3 Who is Judy?
4 Why can't Holly go to the store tomorrow morning?
5 What should Holly take with her to the store?

4 Act out the conversation in groups of four.

Holly	Are there any jobs in the paper?
Archie	Here's one. "Clothing store needs reliable salesperson for Saturday afternoons."
Holly	That sounds perfect! I'll call them now …
Man	Hello, Fashion Fix.
Holly	Oh, hello. I'm calling about the salesperson job. Can I speak to the manager?
Man	You need to speak to Judy, but she just went out. Can I take a message?
Holly	Yes, please. My name's Holly Brightman, and I'm 16 years old. My number is …
Man	Hold on. She just came in. I'll put her on. Just a moment.
Judy	Hello, Holly. What are you doing tomorrow?
Holly	I have a tennis lesson in the morning, but it ends at 12 o'clock. After that, I'm not doing anything.
Judy	Well, let's talk at the store tomorrow afternoon. Bring your résumé!
Holly	Fantastic! I can't wait!

Say it in your language …
That sounds perfect!
I can't wait!

5 Look back at the conversation. Find these expressions.

1 Two ways to say: *Wait a minute.* Hold on.
2 One way to say: *You can talk to her now.*
3 One way to say: *The reason for my call is …*

6 Read the phrases about phone language.

Saying who you are and why you're calling

My name's …/It's …
I'm calling about …
I'd like to/Can I speak to …?

Asking someone to wait

Just a moment.
Hold on, please.

Transferring a call

I'll transfer you now.
I'll put him/her on.

Offering to take a message

Can I take a message?

7 Listen to the conversation. Act out the conversation in pairs.

2.21

Receptionist	Hello. ¹ Penney's Sports Club.
Yasmin	Oh, hello. Can I speak to ² Mr. Ryder, please?
Receptionist	I'm sorry, he's ³ not here at the moment. Can I take a message?
Yasmin	Yes, please. My name's ⁴ Yasmin Hayes. I'm calling about the ⁵ badminton lessons.
Receptionist	Oh, he just came back. I'll transfer you now.
Yasmin	Thank you.

8 Work in pairs. Replace the words in purple in Exercise 7. Use these words and/or your own ideas. Act out the conversations.

1 Pizza Delight / iMart Stores / Hills Garden Center

2 Sarah Morgan / the manager / Ms. Thorne

3 busy / just went out / talking to a customer

4 [your name]

5 job in the kitchen / cashier job / salesperson job

Grammar • Present simple and Present continuous for future

Present simple	Present continuous
The train leaves at 5 o'clock. My tennis lesson ends at 12.	What are you doing tomorrow? I'm meeting my friend for lunch.

Grammar reference page 118

1 Study the grammar table. Choose the correct options to complete the rules.

1 We use the *Present simple / Present continuous* for arrangements.
2 We use the *Present simple / Present continuous* for scheduled events.

2 Choose the correct options.

A ¹*What do you do / What are you doing* on the weekend?
B ²*We visit / We're visiting* our friends in New Orleans, Louisiana.
A ³*Do you fly / Are you flying* there?
B Yes, we ⁴*do / are*. The flight ⁵*departs / is departing* Atlanta at 7 a.m. on Saturday.
A That's early! What time ⁶*does it arrive / is it arriving* in New Orleans?
B It ⁷*gets / is getting* to New Orleans at 8:30.

3 Complete the sentences with the Present simple or Present continuous form of these verbs.

drive	have	open	sing	~~start~~	study

1 Our English exam *starts* at 4 o'clock.
2 The new clothing store .... this afternoon at two o'clock.
3 We .... to our aunt's house tomorrow.
4 My brother .... languages at college in September.
5 I .... a guitar lesson tomorrow after lunch.
6 I .... in a talent contest on Sunday.

4 Invent some exciting plans for tomorrow. Include two definite events. Work in pairs. Tell your partner about your plans.

I'm meeting Robert Pattinson tomorrow evening. We're attending a movie premiere and …

Reading

1 Read the article quickly. Choose the best headline.

1 How to Choose Your Perfect Career
2 Jobs of the Future?
3 The World of Science Fiction

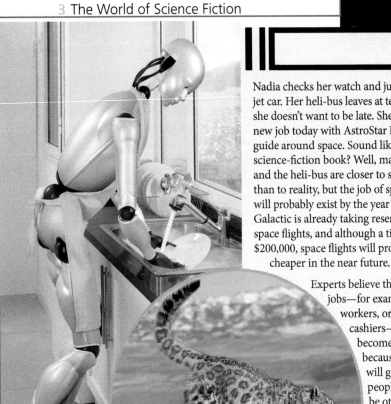

Nadia checks her watch and jumps into her jet car. Her heli-bus leaves at ten o'clock, and she doesn't want to be late. She's starting her new job today with AstroStar Flights, as a tour guide around space. Sound like a page from a science-fiction book? Well, maybe the jet car and the heli-bus are closer to science fiction than to reality, but the job of space tour guide will probably exist by the year 2020. Virgin Galactic is already taking reservations for its space flights, and although a ticket today costs $200,000, space flights will probably get much cheaper in the near future.

Experts believe that some current jobs—for example, call center workers, or supermarket cashiers—will soon become unnecessary because machines will gradually replace people. But there will be other new and exciting jobs in our world of the future. Are you organized, practical and good at paying attention to detail? Then perhaps in 2020 you will be a robot mechanic and maintain and repair the thousands of robots that we will use in our home and working life.

Perhaps you're a great communicator and love talking to people? In the future, online friendships will become as important as real-life friendships, and companies will employ social media managers to maintain their online profiles. If you like working with animals, and you care about the environment, then migration manager might be a good job for you. Migration managers will help to move endangered animals from dangerous habitats to new homes.

But of course, if you're analytical and like looking at statistics and making predictions, then there's already a perfect job for you. You can become a futurologist and predict how our world will develop over the next 20, 30 or 50 years.

Key Words

reality	reservation
social media	endangered
habitat	develop

2 Read the article again. Answer these questions.

2.22

1 Does the job of space tour guide exist now?
   No, it doesn't.
2 How much does a ticket on a Virgin Galactic flight cost?
3 What qualities will a robot mechanic need to have?
4 Why will companies employ social media managers in the future?
5 What will migration managers do?
6 What kind of person might enjoy the job of a futurologist?

Listening

1 Listen to the conversation. Where is Tom going to work?

2.23

a on a boat
b on a ride at a theme park
c in a restaurant

 Listening Bank Unit 5 page 65

2 Discuss the questions.

1 Would you like to work at a theme park? Why?/Why not?
2 What's your ideal summer job?
3 Can you think of any other unusual summer jobs for teenagers?

Writing • An email about plans

1 Read the Writing File.

Writing File *Expressing degrees of certainty*

We can use adverbs of certainty to express how sure we are about a future event.

100% sure
↓
certainly, definitely
probably
maybe, perhaps

certainly, definitely, probably
These adverbs go

- **before** the main verb.
  He definitely lives here.

- **between** the auxiliary and the main verb.
  I'm probably taking a taxi to the airport.

- **after** the verb *to be*.
  She's certainly good at math. Look at her test score!

maybe, perhaps
These adverbs often go at the beginning of the sentence.

- Maybe we'll move to Hawaii next year.

- Perhaps Sarah isn't feeling well.

I think …
We can also use *I think* + subject + verb.

- I think she'll call tomorrow. (but I'm not certain)

2 Make sentences.

1 visit / in / will / We / our / probably / cousins / Kansas City
   We will probably visit our cousins in Kansas City.
2 sister / Maybe / party / your / to / come / the / won't / tomorrow
3 in / definitely / is / Your / closet / bag / the
4 apply / I / for / think / job / I'll / this
5 close / lives / Our / probably / the / to / school / teacher
6 they're / Perhaps / by / traveling / bus

3 Read the email and find the expressions of certainty.

New Message

Hi Judy,
How are you? Are you looking forward to the weekend? I have a lot of plans for this weekend. I'm probably going to go swimming with friends on Saturday morning, and then I think we'll have lunch at this new diner near the park. In the afternoon, my sister and I are taking the train to New York because we have tickets for a Kings of Leon concert at Madison Square Garden! I'm a big fan! I don't know when we'll get back, but my dad will definitely meet us at the station, since it's usually very late.
Maybe we'll go to the park on Sunday morning, but I think I'll be too tired after Saturday night. In the afternoon, we're having a big barbecue. I think the weather will be OK (the forecast is good). I'm going to finish my history project on Sunday evening … my history teacher is probably collecting all the finished projects on Monday morning!
What are you doing this weekend? Tell me about your plans!
Rachel xx

SEND

4 Read the email again and answer the questions.

1 What is Rachel probably going to do before lunch on Saturday? *go swimming with friends*
2 Where is she probably going to have lunch on Saturday?
3 Why are Rachel and her sister traveling to New York on Saturday afternoon?
4 Why is Rachel's dad meeting her at the station on Saturday night?
5 When is Rachel going to finish her history project?

5 You are going to write a reply to Rachel. You can use your real plans for the weekend, or you can make them up. Think about these questions.

- Are you going to hang out with friends?
- What will the weather be like?
- Are you going to play any sports or music?
- Are you going to travel anywhere? If so, how will you get there?

6 Now write your reply. Use your ideas from Exercise 5.

Remember!
- Use expressions of degrees of certainty.
- Use the vocabulary in this unit.
- Check your grammar, spelling and punctuation.

Refresh Your Memory!

Grammar • Review

1 Complete the conversation with *going to* or *will* and the verbs in parentheses.

A ¹ *Are you going to go* (you/go) to the basketball game this afternoon?

B Yes, I ² .... (be). And then I ³ .... (meet) Hailey at the Parrot café.

A Actually, the café's closed this week.

B Then maybe we ⁴ .... (try) the new place in the park.

A I think you ⁵ .... (like) it! The pastries there are delicious.

B I ⁶ .... (buy) one for you there, then.

A Oh, thank you! And don't forget your umbrella! I just saw the weather forecast. It ⁷ .... (rain) later today.

B Well, maybe we ⁸ .... (not go) to the place in the park after all.

2 Make sentences. Use the correct form of the verbs.

1 I / take the train / to New Haven / tomorrow
   I'm taking the train to New Haven tomorrow.
2 The train / leave / at 9:30
3 It / arrive in New Haven / at 11:15
4 I / meet / my friends / at the Franklin Theater
5 We / appear / in a comedy show
6 The show / start / at 12 o'clock
7 It / not finish / until 3:30
8 After the show / we / go / to a party

3 Choose the correct options to complete the text.

I ¹ *'m starting* / *will start* my new job at a clothing store in Washington, DC, tomorrow. I'm really excited! I ² *'m going to get up* / *get up* very early because I don't want to be late on my first day. My train ³ *'s going to leave* / *leaves* at 7:30, and my sister ⁴ *will* / *is going to* drive me to the station. I think I ⁵ *will* / *am going to* enjoy the job because I love fashion, and the store has some beautiful clothes. After work I ⁶ *will meet* / *'m meeting* some friends at a diner near the station. We ⁷ *are having* / *are going to have* a meal together, and I ⁸ *tell* / *will tell* them all about my new job.

Vocabulary • Review

4 Complete the collocations with these words.

answer	attend	check	deal	give	make (x2)
order	prepare	take	work	~~write~~	

1 *write* a report
2 .... a meeting
3 .... some copies
4 .... payments
5 .... office supplies
6 .... with inquiries
7 .... at the front desk
8 .... emails
9 .... a presentation
10 .... the phone
11 .... a spreadsheet
12 .... an appointment

5 Complete the sentences with the correct job qualities.

1 Mary is good at working with groups of people, and she is never late.
   She's a t**eam** p**lay**er and is p**unctua**l.
2 Harry has done this job for ten years, and he is good with computers.
   He is e .... d and has e .... t IT s .... s.
3 Jodie never makes mistakes in her work. She always stays calm and doesn't get angry with other people.
   She is a .... e and p .... t.

Speaking • Review

6 Put the conversation in the correct order.
2.24 **Then listen and check.**

a I'm sorry, she's out at the moment. Can I take a message?
b Hold on, Adam. She's back now. I'll put her on.
c Oh, hello. Can I speak to the manager, please?
d Yes, please. My name's Adam Barnett. I'm calling about the assistant librarian job.
e Hello, Fulton Library. *1*

Dictation

7 Listen and write in your notebook.
2.25

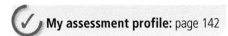
✓ **My assessment profile:** page 142

The Story of Innocent™ Smoothies

Adam Balon, Richard Reed and Jon Wright were friends from college. They all had well-paid jobs, but they also shared a dream. They wanted to start their own company, but they didn't know what *product* to make. They decided to focus on a target *market* that they knew and understood—young people who lived in cities and worked hard. These people wanted to have a healthy lifestyle, but didn't always have the time to prepare healthy food. Adam, Richard and Jon developed some smoothies—fruit juice combined with crushed fruit. But first, they wanted to test their product. So in August 1998, they spent $850 on fruit and sold their smoothies at a local music festival. They hung a big banner over their stand, saying, "Should we quit our jobs to make these smoothies?" Beneath the banner were two trash cans for the empty smoothie bottles, a "Yes" trash can and a "No" trash can.

At the end of the festival, the "Yes" trash can was full of bottles. The friends resigned from their jobs the next day and started up "Innocent Smoothies." Next, they needed some *funding* for their company. They wrote hundreds of letters to possible *investors*, but had no success. However, they kept on trying, and finally Maurice Pinto, a wealthy American, agreed to invest $430,000 in their business.

The rest is history … Innocent Smoothies now sells more than two million bottles of smoothies per week, and it employs over 250 people. Why is it so successful? Adam, Richard and Jon weren't experienced *entrepreneurs*, but they were organized and practical, and they believed in their product. The success of Innocent Smoothies in a big corporate world shows how important personality can be in the success of a business.

Reading

1 **Read the article quickly. Put the events in the correct order.**

   a They sold smoothies at a music festival.
   b They found a wealthy investor.
   c Innocent Smoothies became very successful.
   d They quit their jobs.
   e Adam, Richard and Jon made smoothies. *1*

2 **Read the article again. Find the words in italics that match these definitions.**

   1 people who set up a business *entrepreneurs*
   2 money
   3 something that people make and then sell
   4 people who give money to a business and then take a share of the profit
   5 people who you are selling your product to

3 **Read the article again. Are the statements**
2.26 **true (T) or false (F)?**

   1 Adam, Richard and Jon were friends in college. *T*
   2 Young people who work in cities usually have a healthy lifestyle.
   3 Most people at the festival liked the smoothies.
   4 Adam, Richard and Jon found an investor easily.
   5 Innocent Smoothies is now very successful.

4 **Listen to the marketing expert and complete**
2.27 **the notes.**

The marketing mix: The four Ps

[1] *Product*: is it right for the market? What makes it [2] .... ?

[3] .... : do you want it to be more or less [4] .... than other products?

Promotion: are you going to use [5] .... on TV or in [6] .... ?

[7] .... : do you want to sell your product in [8] .... general stores or in [9] .... designer stores?

My Business Studies File

5 **Work in small groups. Think about a product that you could make and sell. Discuss these questions.**

   • Who/What is your target market?
   • Are there any similar products on the market?
   • How will you find the funding for your business?
   • What do you want your product to look like?

6 **Prepare a presentation for the class about your business idea. Then give your presentation.**

Coast

Vocabulary • Coastal life

Grammar
Passive statements;
Passive questions

Vocabulary
Coastal life; Word building:
Verbs with prefixes
dis- and *re-*

Speaking
Asking for and giving
directions

Writing
A field trip report

Word list page 27
Workbook page 129

1 Match the photos (1–12) to these words. Then listen, check and repeat.
2.28

arcade
beach chair
beach umbrella
cliffs
go-carts
harbor
hot dog stand *1*
ice cream stand
pier
seagull
seawall
souvenir shop

2 Complete the texts with words from Exercise 1.

Unread Message

Hi Jon,

This is my last family vacation ever! A ¹ *seagull* just ate my sandwich, and I have nothing to do! I want to go to the ² .... and buy a postcard, but Mom says that I'll spend all my money. Dad won't let me ride the ³ .... because he says they're too fast, and instead they want to visit the boring ⁴ .... and look at tons of boats!

Oh well—this evening we're going to go to the ⁵ .... for dinner, and maybe I can even get an ice cream cone from the ⁶ ..... So it's not all bad.

Sadie

Gina,

Here's a photo of our new white ⁷ ..... Isn't it lovely? I can sit here on my ⁸ .... and look out at the ocean—I can even see the tall ⁹ .... far away. A lot of people visit the ¹⁰ .... on the ¹¹ ...., where there are tons of games to play. But I prefer the peace and quiet here.

Hope you're well!

Aunt Helen

3 What about you? In pairs, ask and answer.

- Which seaside attractions do you have in your country?
- What do you usually do at the beach?

**Brain Trainer Unit 6
Activities 1 and 2**
Go to page 62

Reading

1 Match the photos (1–4) to the places (A–B). Read the texts quickly and check your answers.

2 Read the texts again. Where can you …

2.29
1 ride a go-cart? *Ocean City*
2 see penguins and whales?
3 see a working harbor?
4 listen to live music?
5 buy some jewelry?
6 go sea kayaking?

3 Read the texts again. Are the statements true (T) or false (F)?

2.29
1 Ocean City is very busy all year round. *F*
2 When the weather is bad, Max and his friends sometimes go to the arcades.
3 Max often goes kite surfing in winter.
4 Kayla probably lives close to the beach.
5 Not many people know about the penguins in Simon's Town.
6 The weather in Simon's Town in winter is better than in many other coastal towns.

4 In pairs, ask and answer.

1 Which place in the texts would you prefer to visit on vacation? Why?
2 Which place would you prefer to live in? Why?
3 How does your hometown change in the different seasons?

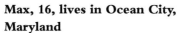

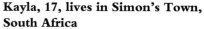

Life in a Seaside Town

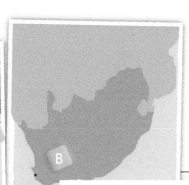

Max, 16, lives in Ocean City, Maryland

In summer, it's crazy living here. Ocean City is a major seaside resort, so we get tons of tourists. All kinds of stores open up along the seafront—ice cream stands, candy stores and places selling cool jewelry and souvenirs. There are also several amusement parks near the beach, with cool rides and go-cart tracks, and a lot of arcades. My friends and I hang out there sometimes and play video games when the weather is not so good. There are also concerts and sand sculpture exhibitions on the beach in summer. The winter is much quieter, and a lot of the summer stores are closed, but the beaches in Ocean City are perfect for kite surfing from October to March. I don't go often because it's expensive, but it's a lot of fun!

Kayla, 17, lives in Simon's Town, South Africa

The amazing thing about Simon's Town is the wildlife. I can walk to the beach in the morning and see whales out in the ocean, and penguins and otters on the beach. There are more than 3,000 African penguins on Boulders Beach, and a lot of tourists come to Simon's Town just to see them! But Simon's Town is also a naval base, and it has a working harbor, so there are always ships coming in and out of the bay. Most places along the Cape Peninsula are wet and windy in the winter, but we're lucky in Simon's Town because it's protected from the winds and rain by the Cape Peninsula mountains. My friends and I often go hiking in winter, and sometimes we go sea kayaking. The sea is too rough for kayaking in summer, but it's calmer in winter, and we can get really close to the whales and seals!

Grammar • Passive statements

The town is protected by the mountains.

The buildings were destroyed by a huge fire.

The work will be finished tomorrow.

Grammar reference page 120

1 Study the grammar table. Choose the correct options to complete the rules.

> 1 Passive sentences start with the person or thing that *does the action / the action happens to*.
> 2 The main verb in passive sentences is always the *infinitive / past participle*.
> 3 We use *by / from* before the agent (the person who or the thing that does the action).

2 Make these sentences passive.

1 Many people admire the beautiful cottages in Cape Cod, Massachusetts.
The beautiful cottages in Cape Cod, Massachusetts, are admired by many people.
2 The owners completely rebuilt their cottage a few years ago.
The cottage .... .
3 They put a new kitchen with a stove in the cottage.
A new kitchen .... .
4 They bought beautiful furniture for the cottage.
Beautiful furniture .... .
5 The owners sold it in 2012 for $380,000.
It was .... .
6 A rich family with two children bought it.
It .... .

🎧 2.30 **Pronunciation Unit 6** page 67

3 Complete the article with the passive form of the verbs.

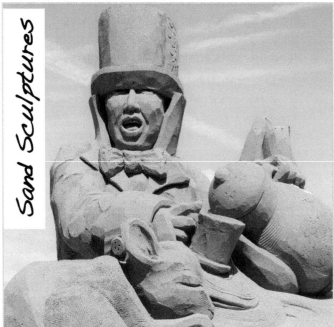

Sand Sculptures

In 2006, in the seaside town of Weston-super-Mare, in England, an amazing sand sculpture of King Kong ¹ *was produced* (produce) by two Dutch sculptors. Twenty tons of sand ² .... (use) to make the sculpture, and it ³ .... (admire) by thousands of visitors. But unfortunately, the sculpture ⁴ .... (destroy) by vandals a month later. The following year, sculptures from different fairy tales, including *Cinderella* and *Alice in Wonderland*, ⁵ .... (create).

The Weston-super-Mare city council is now planning the exhibition for next year. "A new and exciting theme for the exhibition ⁶ .... (announce) next week," said Councilor Jones.

How to make a sand sculpture

Wet sand ⁷ .... (use) to make the sand sculptures. Water ⁸ .... (pour) onto the sand, and then the wet sand ⁹ .... (press) down to remove all the air. Finally, the sand ¹⁰ .... (form) into the right shape.

4 What about you? **Work in pairs. Use the verbs in the box to describe one of these processes.**

add	heat	pour	stir

• how to make a cup of coffee

cut	put	slice	spread

• how to make a cheese and tomato sandwich

Vocabulary • Verbs with prefixes *dis-* and *re-*

 Match these words to the definitions (1–11).
2.31 Then listen, check and repeat.

disagree	disappear *1*	discontinue	discover
dislike	recover	release	remove
replace	research	restore	

1 become lost or impossible to see
2 clean and repair something or give something back to someone
3 take something away
4 stop producing something
5 study a subject in detail
6 become healthy again or bring back something that was lost
7 find
8 have a different opinion than that of another person or people
9 think someone or something is not very nice
10 allow someone to be free or to leave a place
11 take away something or someone and put a new thing there

Word list page 27   **Workbook** page 129

 Study the words and definitions in Exercise 1 again. Choose the correct options.

1 The prefix *dis* / *re* means *again* or *back*.
2 The prefix *dis* / *re* means *not*.

 Complete the sentences with words from Exercise 1.

1 We *researched* the topic of marine archaeology for our history project last week and .... some interesting information.
2 Last week my computer crashed, and all my files .... , but fortunately a computer expert managed to .... most of the information.
3 I don't .... Tanya, but we .... about so many things that we often argue.
4 The old arcades on the pier were .... last month and .... with new 3D machines.
5 My laptop broke down, and I need to .... my files, but the software I have to buy has been .... .
6 A burglar broke into the local pet shop and .... all the animals. The pet shop owner .... them later hiding in the park.

 What about you? **In pairs, ask and answer.**

1 Has anything ever mysteriously disappeared from your room/bag/desk? What?
2 Do you disagree with your parents/brother/sister/friends about any issues? Which?
3 Would you like to research a particular topic in science/history/geography? Why?/Why not?

Brain Trainer Unit 6
Activity 3
Go to page 63

Chatroom Asking for and giving directions

Speaking and Listening

1 Look at the photo. Does Yasmin want to visit the monument? Does Fraser?

2 Listen and read the conversation.
2.32 Check your answers.

3 Listen and read again. Answer the questions.
2.32
1 When was the Pilgrim Monument built?
   between 1907 and 1910
2 What can you do at the Pilgrim Monument?
3 What does Fraser want to do?
4 What does Yasmin want to do?
5 What are Fraser and Yasmin looking for?

4 Act out the conversation in groups of four.

Fraser	Wow, look at that tower! Does your aunt live here, Yasmin?
Yasmin	Don't be silly! This is the Pilgrim Monument.
Fraser	When was it built?
Yasmin	It was built between 1907 and 1910.
Fraser	Are people allowed to visit it?
Yasmin	Yes, of course. There is also a pier and a pirate shipwreck museum just a few blocks from here.
Fraser	Let's go there now. I've been researching pirates for my history project. This is perfect.
Yasmin	Sorry, Fraser. My aunt's expecting us, and we're late and lost. Let's ask for directions.
Fraser	Excuse me, how do we get to Standish Street?
Man	Go past the monument, and then take the second turn on the left. Is that correct?
Woman	No, that's completely wrong! Cross the street in front of the monument. Then turn left and take the first right. You can't miss it.
Yasmin	Thanks so much. Sorry to trouble you!

Say it in your language ...
Don't be silly!
Sorry to trouble you!

5 **Look back at the conversation. Complete the sentences.**

1 Excuse me, *how do we get* to Standish Street?
2 .... the monument.
3 Take the .... on the .... .
4 Cross the street .... .
5 Then .... left, and .... the first right.

 6 **Read the phrases for asking for and giving directions.**

Asking for directions

Excuse me, could you tell me where the post office is?
Excuse me, how do I get to the park?
Excuse me, could you give me directions to the station?

Giving directions

Cross the street next to the bank.
Take the third turn on the left/right.
Turn left/right from here.
Go past the bike store, and then turn left/right.
Take the first left/right.
It's on the left/right.
You can't miss it.

 7 **Listen to the conversation. Act out the conversation in pairs.**
2.33

Holly Excuse me, could you tell me where the movie theater is?
Woman Yes, of course. Turn left at the bookstore and take the first turn on the right. It's across from the coffee shop.
Holly Thank you!

 8 **Look at the map. Work in pairs. Practice giving directions to these places.**

1 supermarket   4 bookstore
2 hospital   5 park
3 drugstore   6 cell phone store

Grammar • Passive questions

Present simple

Are people allowed to visit it?

Where is cocoa produced?

Past simple

When was it built?

Were the buildings restored after the fire?

Future simple

What will be built there in the future?

Will the painting be shown in the art gallery?

Grammar reference page 120

 1 **Study the grammar table. Match the beginnings (1–3) to the endings of the sentences (a–c) to complete the rules.**

1 Present simple questions are formed with
2 Past simple questions are formed with
3 Future simple questions are formed with

a *was/were* + past participle. The subject comes after *was/were*.
b *am/is/are* + past participle. The subject comes after *am/is/are*.
c *will* + *be* + past participle. The subject comes after *will* and before *be*.

2 **Make questions.**

1 pier / was / the / When / built?
   When was the pier built?
2 it / destroyed / How / was?
3 injured / any / in / fire / the / people / Were?
4 new / designed / Will / pier / be / a?
5 the / Are / of / pier / taken / many / photographs?

3 **Listen to the questions and check your answers.**
2.34 **Then listen again and take notes on the answers.**

Reading

 1 Read the article quickly. Write the dates for these events.

1 Blackbeard captured *La Concorde*. *1717*
2 *Queen Anne's Revenge* sank.
3 Blackbeard was killed.
4 The remains of *Queen Anne's Revenge* were discovered.

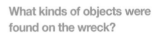

Shipwrecks, Pirates and a Sunken Treasure!

Discover the world of Blackbeard

Today marine archaeologist Thelma Broad tells us about Blackbeard's ship!

Who was Blackbeard?
Blackbeard was a pirate. His real name was Edward Teach, and he lived from 1680 to 1718. In 1717 he captured a French slave ship called *La Concorde*. He renamed the ship *Queen Anne's Revenge*. This then became his main pirate ship,

and he cruised around the Caribbean, attacking other ships and stealing their treasure.

How did *Queen Anne's Revenge* sink?
In May 1718, Blackbeard sailed *Queen Anne's Revenge* from Charleston, South Carolina, in the US, to North Carolina. Here the ship got stuck in the sea floor and sank. Blackbeard was killed a few months later.

When was the wreck of *Queen Anne's Revenge* discovered?
In 1996 a private research company found the remains of *Queen Anne's Revenge* off the coast of North Carolina.

What kinds of objects were found on the wreck?
All kinds of interesting objects were discovered on *Queen Anne's Revenge*, including plates, guns and jewelry. In total, over 16,000 objects were recovered from the wreck between 1997 and 2012, giving us a glimpse into the daily lives and habits of eighteenth-century pirates.

How are the objects cleaned?
It is a very slow process. They have been underwater for such a long time that there is a thick, hard cover around them. Marine archaeologists X-ray the objects in order to find out what is underneath the cover. Then chemicals are used to remove the cover gently. Most objects are put in a chemical bath for about five years!

Have archaeologists discovered any gold?
Yes! Marine archaeologists have found some gold dust, but they haven't found any coins. Blackbeard and his crew probably removed all the coins and other expensive objects before they abandoned the ship.

> **Key Words**
>
> | | | |
> |---|---|---|
> | cruise | stuck | sink |
> | remains | dust | abandon |

 2 Read the article again. Answer the questions.

1 What was Blackbeard's real name?
   Edward Teach
2 What is the connection between *La Concorde* and *Queen Anne's Revenge*?
3 Where did Blackbeard sail in May 1718?
4 Who found the wreck of *Queen Anne's Revenge* in 1996?
5 How many objects were recovered from the wreck between 1997 and 2012?
6 Why weren't there any expensive objects in the wreck?

Listening

 1 Listen to a tour guide talking about the *Cutty Sark*. Choose the best description.

2.36

The *Cutty Sark* was
1 a ship and then a school for sailors.
2 a ship and then a restaurant.
3 a ship and then a home for old sailors.

🎧 **Listening Bank Unit 6** page 65

 2 In pairs, ask and answer.

1 The restoration of the *Cutty Sark* was expensive. Do you think it cost too much?
2 What do you think people can learn about when they visit the *Cutty Sark*?
3 Have you ever visited a historical ship? What was it like?

Writing • A field trip report

 Read the Writing File.

> ### Writing File   Planning a field trip report
>
> **When you write a field trip report, divide your information into clear paragraphs or sections.**
>
> - **Section 1:** Give a brief summary of the basic information: what you did, why, when and where.
> - **Section 2:** Write a description of the trip in clear chronological order.
> - **Section 3:** Use the information from your trip to draw conclusions.

 Look at the sentences. Decide if they come from Section 1, 2 or 3.

Seawall at Goleta Beach

1. In conclusion, we discovered that there are different ways of managing coastal erosion. *3*
2. On Tuesday, October 25, Class 9C traveled to Goleta Beach in California.
3. We looked at the new structures that were built to protect the beach.
4. Our goal was to research coastal erosion and to find out about different ways of managing it.
5. Our first visit in the morning was to Goleta Beach.
6. We also concluded that the use of seawalls in some areas can increase coastal erosion in other areas.

 Use the phrases in the box to complete this field trip report.

In conclusion	In the afternoon, we	~~Our goal was~~
Our first visit	We also concluded	

> On Friday, May 5, Class 10P traveled to Weston-super-Mare. ¹ *Our goal was* to research the redevelopment of the Grand Pier and its impact on tourism.
>
> ² .... was to the Grand Pier. We interviewed the manager of the rebuilt pavilion and found out about the costs of the pier restoration program. ³ .... divided into groups and did surveys of tourists to the town. We asked questions about why they were visiting Weston-super-Mare. We discovered that the main reasons for visiting Weston-super-Mare were the beach, the pier, the arcades and the go-cart track at the pavilion. Some tourists also came for the water sports or to visit relatives.
>
> ⁴ .... , we discovered that although the reconstruction of the pier was very expensive, it was also an important tourist attraction for the town. ⁵ .... that the town could attract more tourists by improving its water sports facilities.

 You are going to write a short field trip report about a visit to an interesting tourist attraction in your country.

Think about
- when it was built
- how many people visit it
- if it was ever damaged or restored

Complete these notes.
Field trip to: ....
Aim: Find out about ....
Conclusion: Is .... a good tourist attraction?

 Now write your report. Use the sample field trip report in Exercise 3 and your notes in Exercise 4.

> ### Remember!
> - Plan your report carefully and divide it into sections.
> - Use the vocabulary in this unit.
> - Check your grammar, spelling and punctuation.

Refresh Your Memory!

Grammar • Review

 Are the sentences active (A) or passive (P)?

1 The Bell Rock Lighthouse was built in 1811. *P*
2 It was designed by Robert Stevenson and John Rennie.
3 They started working on the lighthouse in 1807.
4 It was built of white stone.
5 Stevenson wrote a book about it.
6 People call it Stevenson's Lighthouse.
7 It is still used as a working lighthouse today.

 Make these sentences passive.

1 A builder restored my house.
   My house *was restored by a builder*.
2 They sell delicious food at this store.
   Delicious food .... .
3 We don't keep the bread in this cabinet.
   The bread .... .
4 They will take the photograph this afternoon.
   The photograph .... .
5 Someone stole my bag yesterday.
   My bag .... .
6 A lot of tourists visit this attraction.
   This attraction .... .
7 They won't fix my car this week.
   My car .... .
8 They sent the postcard yesterday.
   The postcard .... .

3 **Make questions. Then match the questions (1–5) to the answers (a–e).**

1 was / *Treasure Island* / When / the / written / book
   When was the book Treasure Island *written?*
2 by / was / written / Who / it
3 a / Was / book / made / into / movie / the
4 lot / Is / today / read / people / it / by / of / a
5 book / sold / is / the / Where

a Yes. It is still read by many people today.
b Robert Louis Stevenson
c In 1883. *1*
d In all good bookstores.
e Yes. The book was made into several movies.

Vocabulary • Review

 Match (1–5) to (a–e) to make words about coastal life.

1 hot   a gull
2 beach   b shop
3 souvenir   c chair
4 go-   d dog stand
5 sea   e carts

 Complete the sentences with the correct form of the verbs.

discontinue	discover	dislike	recover
remove	replace	research	restore

1 You can't buy this cell phone in the stores— it was *discontinued* last year.
2 Could you .... your bag from the chair? I want to sit down.
3 I was sick over the weekend, but I've .... .
4 I want to .... my old bike with a new one.
5 I don't .... Leo, but we're not best friends.
6 Look! I .... $10 in my pocket!
7 My family moved into an old lighthouse last year and .... it.
8 I'm .... my family history at the moment.

Speaking • Review

 Complete the conversation with these phrases.
2.37 **Then listen and check.**

Could you tell me	cross the street	Go past
how do I get to	Turn right	You can't miss it!

A Excuse me. ¹ *Could you tell me* where the station is?
B Yes, of course. It's across from the library. ² ....
A Ah, but ³ .... the library?
B OK. ⁴ .... from here, and then ⁵ .... next to the bookstore. ⁶ .... the school, and then turn left.

Dictation

7 **Listen and write in your notebook.**
2.38

My assessment profile: page 143

Laura Dekker's Profile

Age	Home country
17	The Netherlands

My favorite things …

sailing, surfing, scuba diving, playing the flute

Reading

1 **Read Laura's profile. Look at the photos and the headline. Guess what Laura has achieved.**

a She has written a book about sailing.
b She has designed and made her own boat.
c She has sailed around the world.
d She has built a house shaped like a boat.

2 **Read the article. Answer the questions.**

2.39
1 How old was Laura when her family moved to the Netherlands?
She was four years old.
2 Where did Laura sail on her first solo journey?
3 Why did some people disagree with Laura's plans to sail around the world alone?
4 What was Laura doing when she was found in St. Maarten?
5 How old was Laura when she completed her solo around-the-world trip?
6 What did she eat when she was sailing around the world?

Born to Sail

Laura Dekker was born on a boat and lived there with her parents for the first four years of her life as they completed a seven-year trip around the world. When that journey ended in 1999, Laura's family settled in the Netherlands, but her love of sailing and the ocean grew stronger every day.

When she was six years old, she was given her own boat and learned to sail it. She soon began to make short solo sailing trips. At the age of thirteen, Laura made her first long solo journey from the Netherlands to Britain. Laura then started to plan a journey around the world, but although many people admired her courage and determination, other people disagreed and felt that she was too young to sail alone. The Dutch authorities tried to stop her. "The journey is too dangerous for a thirteen-year-old, and her education will be disturbed," they said. A few months later, Laura ran away from home and was discovered in St. Maarten in the Caribbean. She was trying to buy a boat!

Finally, in July 2010, when Laura was fourteen years old, the Dutch authorities removed the ban on her record-breaking attempt. She began her journey in August 2011, and on January 21, 2012, at sixteen years and four months old, she arrived in St. Maarten and became the youngest person to sail solo around the world.

During her journey, she had to deal with six-meter-high waves, storms and strong winds. She lived on a diet of pasta, rice, crackers and pancakes. She kept her boat and herself safe from bad weather and also from pirates, and she even did some homework as well!

Class discussion

1 What do you think? Was Laura too young to sail solo around the world?
2 How do you think Laura felt during her journey? Why?
3 Would you like to do what Laura did? Why?/Why not?
4 What would you miss most if you sailed around the world?

Review 2

Grammar • Modals: ability, obligation, prohibition, advice

1 **Complete the second sentence so that it means the same as the first. Use the verbs given. There may be more than one possible answer.**

1 It's not necessary to wear a helmet when you ride a scooter.
You *don't have to wear a helmet* when you ride a scooter.
2 I advise you to take some food to the party.
You …. to the party.
3 It's a bad idea to forget your sister's birthday.
You …. sister's birthday.
4 Leave your bags outside the classroom!
You …. outside the classroom.
5 No talking in the library!
We …. in the library.
6 She is able to play the guitar, but she isn't able to play the piano.
She …. the guitar, but she …. the piano.

• Past modals

2 **Put these sentences into the past tense.**

1 Sarah can't read well without her glasses.
Sarah couldn't read well without her glasses.
2 We have to take the dog for a walk.
3 They don't have to study over summer break.
4 I can hear you, but I can't see you.
5 They must be at the theater at 6 o'clock.

• Modals: possibility

3 **Choose the correct options.**

A Is this John's bag?
B No, it ¹ *can't / could* be John's bag. John's bag is blue, and this one is red.
A Well, it ² *must / could* be Henry's bag. His is red.
B Yes, it ³ *could / can't* be Henry's, or it ⁴ *might / must* be Jade's. Her bag is red, too.
A Let's look inside. Aha, this book has Jade's name in it.
B So it ⁵ *must / can't* be Jade's bag!

• Will/Going to

4 **Choose the correct options.**

1 A I'm hungry.
B I'*m going to / 'll* make you a sandwich.
2 A What *are you going to / will you* do over the summer break?
B We'*re going to / will* sail the ocean!
3 Oh no! It's 8 o'clock already. We'*re going to / will* miss the bus.
4 A Where do you think you *are going to / will* live in 2020?
B I think I'*m going to / 'll* live on my own private island!
5 A *Are you going to / Will you* go to Amy's birthday party tonight?
B Yes, I *am / will*. How about you?
A No, I can't. But I've already sent her a card.

5 **Complete the sentences with *will* or *going to* and the verbs in parentheses.**

1 I think my team *will win* (win) the next game.
2 My friends and I …. (meet) at the movie theater tomorrow at 5 o'clock, but I don't know which movie we …. (see) yet.
3 A Oh no! The car's not working.
B Don't worry. We …. (take) the bus to school.
4 I broke my brother's new cell phone.
He …. (be) really angry with me!
5 What …. (study) in college next year?

• Present simple and Present continuous for future

6 **Complete the text with the Present simple or Present continuous form of the verbs in parentheses.**

I'm looking forward to tomorrow—I have a lot of plans. My singing lesson ¹ *starts* (start) at 9 a.m., and it ² …. (end) at 10:30 a.m. Then I ³ …. (meet) my friends in the park. In the afternoon, we ⁴ …. (take) a train to Philadelphia. The train ⁵ …. (leave) at 3:30 p.m. We ⁶ …. (visit) the Rodin Museum, and then we ⁷ …. (go) to the theater in the evening. What ⁸ …. (you/do) tomorrow?

Passive statements

7 **Make these sentences passive.**

1 People make chocolate from cacao beans.
Chocolate *is made from cacao beans*.
2 They produce Sony computers in Japan.
Sony computers .... .
3 They won't clean your windows tomorrow.
Your windows .... .
4 Someone broke this plate yesterday.
This plate .... .
5 Van Gogh didn't paint the *Mona Lisa*.
The *Mona Lisa* .... .
6 People will discover new sources of energy
in the future.
New sources of energy .... .

8 **Complete the text with the correct passive form of the verbs in parentheses.**

In the past, most clothes [1] *were made* (make)
out of natural materials like leather or cotton,
and they [2] .... (sew) by hand at home. Now man-
made materials like polyester [3] .... (use), and most
clothes [4] .... (make) in factories. Who knows how
our clothes [5] .... (produce) in the future? Perhaps
new materials [6] .... (discover).

Passive questions

9 **Make these questions passive.**

1 Who makes this beautiful jewelry?
Who is this beautiful jewelry made by?
2 When did they set up the company?
3 Does your teacher check your homework?
4 Will they decorate your room on Tuesday?
5 How did they find the shipwreck?

10 **Make passive questions for these answers.
Use the question words.**

1 My bag is made of leather and metal. (What)
What is your bag made of?
2 This house was built in 1910. (When)
3 The book will be published by Penguin
Books. (Who)
4 The poem was written by Pablo Neruda. (Who)
5 These flowers are grown in Holland. (Where)

Speaking • Asking for clarification

1 **Put the conversation in the correct order.**

☐ a Oh, I see! Thanks.
☐ b Yes, I know. But all the streets are closed
to traffic today.
[1] c We can't take the bus to the community
center today.
☐ d No, the bike race is on the streets! But we
can walk to the community center.
☐ e What do you mean? We always go by bus.
☐ f It's because of the bike race.
☐ g Are you saying that there's a bike race
at the community center?
☐ h Sorry, I don't understand. Why are
the streets closed?

Phone language

2 **Choose the correct options to complete
the conversation.**

A Hello, Redhill Bookstore, can I help you?
B Hello, [1] *I'd like* / *I like* to speak to the
manager, please.
A I'm sorry, he's talking to a customer at the
moment. [2] *Can* / *Do* I take a message?
B Yes, please. My name's Emma Moore.
I'm calling [3] *after* / *about* the salesperson job.
A Oh, the manager's free now. [4] *Hold* / *Wait* on,
please. I'll [5] *transfer* / *put* you to him now.

Asking for and giving directions

3 **Complete the conversations with these phrases.**

can't miss	Cross	~~give me directions~~
Go past	how do I	on the right
the second turn	turn left	

A Excuse me, could you [1] *give me directions*
to the library?
B Yes, of course. [2] .... the street next to the school.
Then take [3] .... on the right. It's [4] .... .
A Thank you so much.

A Excuse me, [5] .... get to the park?
B [6] .... the bank, and then [7] .... . You [8] .... it.
A Thank you.

Vocabulary • Natural disasters

1 **Complete the words for natural disasters.**

1 ts*unam*i
2 f_m _ _ e
3 dr _ _ _ ht
4 e _ _ t_qu _ _ e
5 fl _ _ d
6 a_a _ _ _ ch_
7 h _ r _ _ _ _ _ e
8 di_ea _ _

• Phrasal verbs 2

2 **Complete the sentences with these words.**

across	down (x2)	forward to
~~off~~	~~on~~	on
out (x2)	through	

1 It was very hot, so I took *off* my sweater and put *on* some sunscreen.
2 If your car breaks .... on the highway or runs .... of gas, you should call for roadside assistance.
3 If you stop panicking and calm .... , we will be able to get .... this situation without an accident.
4 I came .... an interesting article in the newspaper a few days ago.
5 Are you looking .... your vacation next week?
6 Let's keep .... trying to fix this engine—I'm sure we can figure .... what's wrong with it.

• Work collocations

3 **Choose the correct options.**

1 *answer* / *prepare* the phone
2 *make* / *take* an appointment
3 *check* / *work* at the front desk
4 *deal* / *make* some copies
5 *prepare* / *give* a spreadsheet
6 *attend* / *write* a report
7 *deal* / *attend* a meeting
8 *order* / *give* a presentation
9 *check* / *attend* emails
10 *take* / *answer* payments
11 *give* / *order* office supplies
12 *give* / *deal* with inquiries

• Job qualities

4 **Read the sentences (1–4) and then match two descriptions from the box to each name.**

excellent IT skills	experienced	good communicator
~~patient~~	practical	punctual
~~reliable~~	team player	

Jim: *patient, reliable*　　**Dan:** .... , ...
Helen: .... , ...　　**Kerry:** .... , ...

1 Jim doesn't get angry easily, and you can always trust him.
2 Helen is never late, and she can do useful things.
3 Dan is good at using a computer, and he likes working with other people.
4 Kerry has had this job for ten years, and she is good at talking to people.

• Coastal life

5 **Complete the words.**

1 You can buy presents for your friends in a s*ouveni*r shop.
2 A common coastal bird is a s _ _ g _ ll.
3 You can sit in a b _ _ _ h c _ _ _ r on the beach.
4 If you're hungry, you can buy a h_t d _ _ and then go to an i_e cr _ _ m s _ _ nd.
5 There is often an ar _ _ d_ near the pi _ _ .
6 Get some shade under a b _ _ ch u _ _ _ _ _ la.

• Verbs with prefixes *dis-* and *re-*

6 **Match the verbs (a–h) to the definitions (1–8).**

1 think someone is wrong *b*
2 allow someone to leave a place
3 find something
4 take something away from somewhere
5 find out information about something
6 not like someone/something
7 get better
8 stop making something

a research　　　　e release
b disagree　　　　f discover
c dislike　　　　　g recover
d remove　　　　　h discontinue

Word list

Unit 4 • Survive!

Natural disasters

avalanche	/ˈævəˌlæntʃ/
bury	/ˈbɛri/
destroy	/dɪˈstrɔɪ/
disease	/dɪˈziz/
drought	/draʊt/
drown	/draʊn/
earthquake	/ˈɚθkweɪk/
erupt	/ɪˌrʌpt/
famine	/ˈfæmɪn/
flood	/flʌd/
hurricane	/ˈhɚɪˌkeɪn, ˈhʌr-/
spread	/sprɛd/
starve	/starv/
survive	/səˈvaɪv/
tsunami	/tsʊˈnami/
volcano	/vɑlˈkeɪnoʊ/

Phrasal verbs 2

break down	/ˌbreɪk ˈdaʊn/
calm down	/ˌkɑm ˈdaʊn/
come across	/ˌkʌm əˈkrɔs/
figure out	/ˌfɪgyɚ ˈaʊt/
get through	/ˌgɛt ˈθru/
keep on	/ˌkip ˈɔn/
look forward to	/ˌlʊk ˈfɔrwɚd tə/
put on	/ˈpʊt ˈɔn/
run out of	/ˌrʌn ˈaʊt əv/
take off	/ˌteɪk ˈɔf/

Unit 5 • Work for It

Work collocations

answer the phone	/ˈænsɚ ðə ˈfoʊn/
attend a meeting	/əˌtɛnd ə ˈmiʔ ɪŋ/
check emails	/ˌtʃɛk ˈimeɪlz/
deal with inquiries	/ˌdil wɪð ɪnˈkwaɪəriz/
give a presentation	/ˌgɪv ə prɛzənˈteɪʃən/
make an appointment	/ˌmeɪk ən əˈpɔɪntˀmənt/
make some copies	/ˌmeɪk səm ˈkɑpiz/
order office supplies	/ˌɔrdɚ ˈɔfɪs səˌplaɪz/
prepare a spreadsheet	/prɪˌpɛr ə ˈsprɛdʃit/

take payments	/ˌteɪk ˈpeɪmənts/
work at the front desk	/ˈwɚk ət ðə ˌfrʌnt ˈdɛsk/
write a report	/ˌraɪt ə rɪˈpɔrt/

Job qualities

accurate	/ˈækyərɪt/
analytical	/ˌænlˈɪt ɪkəl/
excellent IT skills	/ˈɛksələnt ˌaɪ ˈti ˌskɪlz/
experienced	/ɪkˈspɪriənst/
good communicator	/ˌgʊd kəˈmyunəˌkeɪtɚ/
leadership qualities	/ˈlidɚˌʃɪp ˈkwɑləʔ iz/
organized	/ˈɔrgəˌnaɪzd/
patient	/ˈpeɪʃənt/
practical	/ˈpræktɪkəl/
punctual	/ˈpʌŋktʃuəl/
reliable	/rɪˈlaɪəbəl/
team player	/ˈtim ˌpleɪɚ/

Unit 6 • Coast

Coastal life

arcade	/arˈkeɪd/
beach chair	/ˈbitʃ tʃɛr/
beach umbrella	/ˈbitʃ ʌmˈbrɛlə/
cliffs	/klɪfs/
go-cart	/ˈgoʊkart/
harbor	/ˈharbɚ/
hot dog stand	/ˈhat dɔg ˈstænd/
ice cream stand	/ˈaɪs krim ˈstænd/
pier	/pɪr/
seagull	/ˈsigʌl/
seawall	/ˈsiwɔl/
souvenir shop	/ˌsuvəˈnɪr ˈʃɑp/

Verbs with prefixes *dis-* and *re-*

disagree	/ˌdɪsəˈgri/
disappear	/ˌdɪsəˈpɪr/
discontinue	/ˌdɪskənˈtɪnyu/
discover	/dɪˈskʌvɚ/
dislike	/dɪsˈlaɪk/
recover	/rɪˈkʌvɚ/
release	/rɪˈlis/
remove	/rɪˈmuv/
replace	/rɪˈpleɪs/
research	/ˈrisɚtʃ, rɪˈsɚtʃ/
restore	/rɪˈstɔr/

7 Final Frontiers

Grammar
First and Second conditional;
Subject/Object questions

Vocabulary
Adjective antonyms; Space

■ **Speaking**
Giving warnings

■ **Writing**
An application letter

Word list page 61
Workbook page 130

Vocabulary • Adjective antonyms

1 **Match the words in the first box to the opposite words in the second box. Some words can make two pairs. Then listen, check and repeat.**
3.1

ancient *modern*	deep	light	low
narrow	ordinary	permanent	weak

dark	heavy
high	~~modern~~
powerful	shallow
strange	strong
temporary	wide

2 **Complete the sentences with words from Exercise 1.**

1 "Can you carry it?" "No, it's too *heavy*. My arms aren't *strong* enough."
2 The plane has a very .... engine, so it can go really fast and really .... up in the sky.
3 Green Street is our .... address. We're moving to our .... home next month.
4 I love the new, ... buildings in Beijing and also the .... ones that were built 600 years ago.
5 The river is .... here. Over there it's too .... to cross.
6 The baby bird is very .... . We think it might die.
7 "Why is he wearing purple pants? He looks really .... ." "He isn't wearing his .... clothes because he's doing a comedy show today."
8 The water in the lake is .... . Children play in it, but you can't swim because it isn't .... enough.
9 In summer, it's still .... at ten o'clock at night, because the sun goes down very late. But in winter, it gets .... at four in the afternoon.
10 The wall's .... , so it's safe to jump over it.

3 **In pairs, describe the photos. Use adjectives from Exercise 1.**

The cave in photo 4 is dark, deep and narrow.

 3.2, 3.3 **Pronunciation Unit 7 page 67**

 **Brain Trainer Unit 7 Activities 1 and 2** Go to page 63

Reading

1 Look at the photos. What can you see in them?

2 Read the article quickly. Match the headings (1–3) to the paragraphs (A–C).

1 A world of water
2 New plants, new people
3 Underground secrets

3 Read the article again. Answer the questions.

1 How did people discover a new rain forest?
With the help of Google Earth ™.
2 Why does the text mention the number 30,000?
3 Why is it useful to make contact with rain forest tribes?
4 What might you find in a cave? List three things.
5 Why are there underwater cities?
6 What is useful when you are exploring underwater? Why?

4 What about you? **Ask and answer in pairs.**

1 Would you like to explore these places? Why?/Why not?
2 Where else can we explore?
3 Do you think it's better to be an explorer today or an explorer in the past? Why?

Explorers: Where Next?

The explorers of the past were the first to see new continents, reach the poles or sail around the world. But what on earth can the people of tomorrow discover?

A ....

The biggest rain forest in southern Africa was discovered in Mozambique only a few years ago, with the help of Google Earth™. Perhaps there are other unknown rain forests waiting for discovery. There are probably about thirty thousand species of rain forest plants and animals that we know nothing about. There are also rain forest tribes that have had no contact with the modern world.

If we were friends with these tribes, we would probably know a lot more about medicinal plants. There's definitely more to discover in the rain forests.

B ....

In the US alone, people find about 1,000 new caves every year. In fact, we know more about Mars than about the underground places on Earth! You'd soon discover something exciting if you spent a lot of time spelunking: a strange new animal species, or some beautiful crystal flowers, or even an ancient painting.

C ....

You'll have a good chance of discovering something new if you look in the oceans. There are ancient cities which have disappeared underwater after earthquakes and floods. There are canyons six times deeper than the Grand Canyon and more active volcanoes beneath the sea than above it. If you want to see something down there, you'll need a strong light, because below 200 meters, it's completely dark. But we have only explored about five percent of the earth's oceans. There's a lot more to find!

Grammar • First and Second conditional

First conditional
If you want to see something, you'll need a strong light.

Second conditional
If we were friends with these tribes, we would know a lot more.

Grammar reference page 122

 Study the grammar table. Copy and complete the table with these words.

> impossible   past   possible   ~~present~~   will   would

	First conditional	Second conditional
if clause	¹ *Present* simple	² .... simple
main clause	³	⁴ ....
use	⁵ .... situations in the future	unlikely or ⁶ .... situations in the present or future

 Choose the correct options.

1 If you *explore / will explore* the oceans, you'll find some amazing fish.
2 The camera will take photos of the ocean floor if it *doesn't break / won't break* in the deep water.
3 He *is / will be* happy if he finds a new species.
4 If we *dive / will dive* below 200 meters, the water will be completely dark.
5 We *don't see / won't see* anything if we don't bring flashlights.
6 If you scream, people *hear / will hear* you.

③ **Complete the sentences with the correct form of the verbs.**

1 If I were a climber, I *would want* (want) to climb Machapuchare ("Fish Tail Mountain") in Nepal.
2 However, I would get into trouble if the Nepalese .... (find) me there.
3 According to their beliefs, the god Shiva .... (not like) it if someone climbed up to his sacred home.
4 If the Nepalese .... (not have) these beliefs, people would try to climb Machapuchare.
5 If anyone reached the top, they .... (see) a view that no one has ever seen before.

 Complete the email with the correct form of the verbs. Use the First or Second conditional.

New Message

Hi Lily,
I'm in Antarctica! I'd be cold if I ¹ *didn't have* (not have) the right equipment, but I'm OK in my warm coat. If you ² .... (be) here, you'd love it!
We ³ .... (start) our journey to the ice caves tomorrow if there isn't too much wind. If we ⁴ .... (reach) the caves, I'll take a lot of photos.
I ⁵ .... (prefer) it if I had my big camera with me, but if I packed it in my bag, there ⁶ .... (not be) any space for my clothes! I hope my little camera will work OK. If we ⁷ .... (be) lucky with the weather, we'll stay at the caves for two weeks. The Internet ⁸ .... (not work) there if the weather is bad, but I'll send another email as soon as I can.
Love,
Adam

 Complete the sentences so they are true for you.

1 I'd be really scared if …
2 My parents would worry if …
3 My friends will be really happy if …
4 If I arrived at school an hour late, …

 Complete the questions with the correct form of these verbs.

> ask   can   choose   ~~do~~   give

1 If it's sunny this weekend, what *will you do* (you)?
2 If you .... go to any country in the world, where would you go?
3 If you had to learn a new sport, which sport .... (you)?
4 If someone .... you some money for your birthday, what will you spend it on?
5 If you were in trouble, who .... (you) for help?

⑦ **Work in pairs. Ask and answer the questions in Exercise 6.**

> If it's sunny this weekend, I'll probably go to the beach.

Vocabulary • Space

1 Match these words to the items in the picture (1–12). Then listen, check and repeat.

3.5

asteroid	astronaut	astronomer	comet *1*
galaxy	moon	orbit	planet
solar system	spacecraft	~~star~~	telescope

Word list page 61 **Workbook** page 130

2 Complete the sentences with words from Exercise 1.

1 I can see thousands of *stars* in the sky tonight.
2 A .... is a large group of stars.
3 Mars is a .... in our solar system.
4 An .... is smaller than a planet. Sometimes these objects crash into Earth.
5 Earth is one of the eight planets in our .... .
6 You will need a .... to see the planets clearly.
7 An .... is a person who studies space.
8 In the night sky, a .... looks like a star with a tail.
9 An .... is a person who travels into space.
10 A planet's .... is its path around the sun.
11 The .... creates the biggest light in the sky at night.
12 Astronauts travel through space in a .... .

Brain Trainer Unit 7
Activity 3
Go to page 63

3 Take the quiz. Then check your answers in the box below.

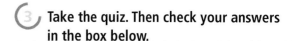

SPACE QUIZ

****
TEST YOUR SPACE KNOWLEDGE!
****

TRUE (T) OR FALSE (F)?

1 Earth's orbit around the sun takes one month. *F*

2 Venus is the biggest planet in our solar system.

3 There are billions of galaxies, and each galaxy has at least ten million stars.

4 A star is a sun in a different solar system from our own.

5 The first astronaut went to Mars in 1989.

6 The most powerful telescope on Earth is in the desert in Chile.

7 The planet Jupiter has 63 moons.

8 There are rings around the planet Neptune.

9 We last saw Halley's Comet without a telescope in 1986, and we will see it next in 2061.

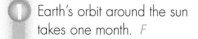

1 F (It takes one year.) **2** F (Jupiter) **3** T **4** T
5 F (No astronauts have been to Mars.) **6** T **7** T
8 F (Saturn) **9** T

Speaking and Listening

1 **Look at the photo. Answer the questions.**

1 What did Fraser get for his birthday?
2 What can Yasmin see?
3 Why are Archie and Fraser laughing?

2 **Listen and read the conversation.**
3.6 **Check your answers.**

3 **Listen and read again. Answer the questions.**
3.6
1 Where did the telescope come from?
It was Fraser's birthday present from his uncle.
2 What is Fraser's uncle's job?
3 What might make you blind?
4 Is it daytime or nighttime?
5 What does Yasmin think she can see in the telescope?
6 What can she really see?

4 **Act out the conversation in groups of three.**

Yasmin	What did you get for your birthday, Fraser?
Fraser	Come and see.
Archie	Wow! A telescope! Who gave it to you?
Fraser	My uncle. He's an astronomer.
Archie	Cool job! What does he study?
Fraser	Comets, I think.
Archie	Can I look through the telescope?
Fraser	OK, but make sure you don't break it. And be careful not to look at the sun with it.
Archie	Why? What happens?
Fraser	It damages your eyes. You might even go blind.
Yasmin	Chill out, Fraser! That shouldn't be a problem now. It's dark outside. Can I take a look?
Fraser	Sure. But I wouldn't press the red button if I were you. It changes the direction of the …
Yasmin	Wow! I can see an orange planet really clearly. This is incredible!
Fraser	Yasmin! That's my lamp!
Yasmin	Oh! Uh … I knew that!

Say it in your language …
Chill out!
This is incredible!

5 **Look back at the conversation. Complete these sentences.**

1 *Make sure* you don't break it.
2 .... not to look at the sun with it.
3 I wouldn't press the red button if I ....

 6 **Read the phrases for giving warnings.**

Make sure you don't …
Watch out for the …
Be careful not to …
I wouldn't … if I were you.

 7 **Listen to the conversations. What dangers do the speakers mention? Act out the conversations in pairs.**

3.7

Fraser I'm going to ¹ take my telescope to the park.
Yasmin OK, but I wouldn't ² go there alone at night if I were you. It's dangerous. And make sure you don't ³ forget your flashlight.

Holly I'm going to ⁴ learn to scuba dive.
Archie That sounds like fun, but watch out for ⁵ sharks! And be careful not to ⁶ stay underwater too long.

 8 **Work in pairs. Replace the words in purple in Exercise 7. Use these words and/or your own ideas. Act out the conversations.**

> I'm going to sail across the Atlantic.

> OK, but I wouldn't …

1 sail across the Atlantic / work for NASA / go to the North Pole

2 do it on your own / become an astronaut / go there in winter

3 fall out of the boat / crash any spacecraft / forget your gloves

4 climb a mountain / go spelunking / go on a space flight

5 avalanches / scary bats / aliens

6 fall off a cliff / get lost underground / open the window

Grammar • Subject/Object questions

What happens if I press this button?
Who gave it to you?

What does he do all day?
What did you get for your birthday?

Grammar reference page 122

 1 **Study the grammar table. Complete the rules with *subject* or *object*.**

1 When the question word is the .... of the sentence, we make questions with: question word + *do/does/did* + subject + infinitive without *to*.
2 When the question word is the .... of the sentence, we make questions with: question word + Present/Past/Future form of the verb. We don't use *do/does/did*.

 2 **Are these object questions (O) or subject questions (S)? Complete the questions.**

1 What *do you want* (you/want) to watch? *O*
2 How many people .... (study) English at your school?
3 What .... (that word/mean)?
4 Who .... (go) to the astronomy club on Fridays?
5 Who .... (drive) you to school in the morning?
6 Who .... (we/know) in Washington, DC?

 3 **Make questions. Match them to these answers.**

| a kangaroo | ~~Canada~~ | chocolate |
| Marco Polo | Roald Amundsen | the US |

1 Which country / Leif Eriksson / discover / in the 11th century? *Canada*
2 Who / travel / in China / in the 13th century?
3 What / Hernan Cortes / bring / to Europe / in 1528?
4 What / come / to Europe / on the ship of James Cook / in 1770?
5 Which country / Lewis and Clark / explore / at the beginning of the 19th century?
6 Who / reach / the South Pole / first?

Reading

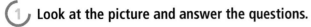

1 **Look at the picture and answer the questions.**

If humans started a colony on Mars,
1 would it be easy to spend time outside?
2 how would they build things?
3 where would they live?
4 how would they grow food?

NEXT STOP: MARS

No astronauts have walked on the moon since 1972, but some people think that the days of humans on other planets are not far away. In twenty years, there might even be a permanent colony on Mars.
We asked astronomer Matthew Simmons to tell us more.

What makes Mars a good place for a colony in space?
Of all the planets in our solar system, Mars is the most suitable for human life. A day on Mars is a similar length to our own: 24 hours and 40 minutes. If you lived on Venus, a day would last 243 Earth days! Mars also has seasons like those on Earth. There is ice on Mars too, so if there were colonists there, they would be able to make water.

What problems would the colonists have?
One big problem would be the cold. Mars has an average temperature of -63°C. There's also weaker gravity than on Earth, more radiation from the sun and much less oxygen.

So how would people survive?
Robots would build underground homes before the colonists arrived. There would be big greenhouses too, and these would have a temperature warm enough to grow plants. Perhaps we could send spacecraft full of greenhouse gases to Mars, and over time, change the temperature and atmosphere of the whole planet so it was more like Earth.

How long does the journey to Mars take?
About nine months. But if you went, you'd probably have to stay on Mars for the rest of your life.

No one would volunteer to be a colonist if they could never come home again! Interestingly, that's not true. When a space magazine wrote about a future colony on Mars, it got letters from more than 400 people who wanted to be part of it.

> **Key Words**
>
> colony/colonist   gravity
> radiation   oxygen
> greenhouse   atmosphere

2 **Read the article quickly and check your answers to Exercise 1.**

3 **Read the article again. Answer the questions.**

3.8
1 Where in space might humans live in the near future? *They might live on Mars.*
2 What is there on Mars that makes it more suitable for human life than other planets?
3 Unfortunately, Mars has a lot more of this than Earth. What is it?
4 How might Mars change in the future?
5 How long would colonists stay on Mars?
6 If there were a colony on Mars, would anyone volunteer to go to it?

4 **Find these numbers in the article. Explain what they refer to.**

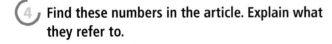
| ~~1972~~ | 20 | 243 | -63 | 9 | 400 |

The last person on the moon was there in 1972.

Listening

1 **You are going to listen to some ideas of other places where people might build colonies in the future. What places might the speakers mention?**

2 **Listen to speakers A, B and C. Which types of colonies do they talk about?**
3.9
A ....
B ....
C ....

> **Listening Bank Unit 7** page 66

3 **What about you?** **In pairs, ask and answer the questions.**

1 Would you like to be a colonist on Mars or in any of the places in Exercise 2? Why?/Why not?
2 What kind of person would be a good colonist in each of these places?

Writing • An application letter

 Read the Writing File.

Writing File   Letter writing

- If you don't know the name of the person who you are writing to, start with *Dear Sir/Madam.*
- Write the subject of the letter as a heading.
- Give the reason for writing: *I was very interested to see …, I am writing to …*
- In the last paragraph, say what you want to happen next: *I very much hope that you …, I look forward to hearing from you.*
- End with *Sincerely, Yours truly,* or *Regards,* and your name.

 Read the job ad and application letter. Find language from the Writing File.

Colonists needed

New Frontiers is looking for people to start two exciting new colonies, one on the ocean floor and the other on Mars.

Dear Sir/Madam,

Underwater colony

I was very interested to see your ad. I am writing to apply for a job as an underwater colonist. I have always loved the water, and for many years it has been my dream to find out more about life in the ocean. There are more people and less wildlife in my local area every year. If I lived in an underwater colony, I would be closer to nature, and I would love that.

If I lived in the colony, I would be a useful member of the team. I am a hardworking and flexible person, and I am a good communicator. My favorite hobby is scuba diving, so I already have a lot of experience being underwater. I have never dived in dark water, but I learn new skills quickly.

I very much hope that you will choose me as a colonist. I look forward to hearing from you.

Yours truly,
Jasmine Wilkins
Jasmine Wilkins

 Read the letter again. Answer the questions.

1 Which colony is Jasmine applying for?
   the underwater colony
2 What is her dream?
3 What would she like about living in the colony?
4 What kind of person is she?
5 What useful experience does she have?

 Fill in the blanks in the reply to Jasmine's letter.

Underwater colony

¹ *Dear* Jasmine,

I was ² …. to read your application letter. I would like to invite you to an interview at our office at 2 p.m. on Thursday, May 5.

I ³ …. much ⁴ …. that you can come to the interview. I look ⁵ …. to ⁶ …. from you.

Yours ⁷ …. ,

Michael de Souza

 Look back at the article on page 34. Which things would be useful if you lived in a colony on Mars?

1 I go horseback riding every weekend. ✗
2 I have done a lot of spelunking.
3 I have often helped on my family's farm.
4 I have excellent IT skills.
5 I'm practical and reliable.

 You are going to write a letter applying to be a Mars colonist. Take notes about yourself. Use the questions in Exercise 3 to help you.

Write your letter. Use the outline below and your notes from Exercise 6.

1 Opening *Dear Sir/Madam,*
2 Give the reason for writing.
3 Say why the job interests you.
4 Describe your skills, personality and experience.
5 Say what you want to happen next.
6 Closing *Regards*

Remember!
- Only include skills, personality qualities and experiences that might be useful for the job.
- Use phrases from the Writing File.
- Use vocabulary and grammar from this unit.
- Check your grammar, spelling and punctuation.

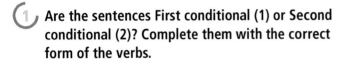

Grammar • Review

1 Are the sentences First conditional (1) or Second conditional (2)? Complete them with the correct form of the verbs.

1 If astronauts went to Venus, they *wouldn't survive* (not survive) the 465°C temperatures. *2*
2 We .... (be) out almost all day if we visit the space museum.
3 If we .... (find) intelligent life on other planets, will it be good or bad news for humans?
4 I'd look at the stars every night if I .... (have) a telescope.
5 What .... (you/do) if you met an alien?
6 She .... (not get) a job at NASA if she doesn't do well on her science exams.

2 Make answers. Use the First or Second conditional.

1 Should I tell Mel? (no / she / tell / everyone)
   No. If you tell Mel, she'll tell everyone.
2 Are you getting a job? (yes / I / have / more money)
3 Is he from Chile? (no / he / speak / Spanish)
4 Can we go to Egypt? (probably / we / see / some amazing ancient buildings)
5 Do you like meat? (no / I / not be / a vegetarian)

3 Complete the questions in the conversation. Use the correct form of the verbs in bold.

Harry	Lucy **learned** to scuba dive last week.
Grandma	Who ¹ *learned* to scuba dive?
Harry	Lucy. She **had** a nice instructor for her course.
Grandma	Who ² .... for her course?
Harry	A nice instructor. But on her first dive, she **broke** her arm on the side of the boat.
Grandma	What ³ .... ?
Harry	Her arm.
Grandma	Oh no! Is she OK?
Harry	Yes. Her diving instructor **helped** her.
Grandma	Who ⁴ .... her?
Harry	Her instructor. And he **sent** flowers to Lucy every day after that!
Grandma	What ⁵ ....?
Harry	Flowers. She **got** flowers from him.
Grandma	Who ⁶ .... flowers?
Harry	Lucy!

Vocabulary • Review

4 Complete the sentences with these words.

heavy	low	modern	narrow
ordinary	~~shallow~~	temporary	weak

1 The water's *shallow*. It's only up to my knees.
2 We can't pass that car. The road is too .... .
3 I can't carry your bag. It's too .... .
4 He has a .... job until the end of the summer.
5 It was an .... day, just like every other day.
6 She's very .... because she hasn't eaten for weeks.
7 The cliffs are pretty .... , so they're easy to climb.
8 It's a .... building. It was built two years ago.

5 Write the antonyms of the adjectives in Exercise 4.

shallow – deep

6 Complete the sentences with appropriate words.

1 What stars can you see through a *telescope*?
2 I want to be an a.... and travel in a s.... .
3 Is that a c.... in the sky? Look at its bright tail!
4 Saturn is in the same s.... s.... as Earth.
5 Our g.... has millions of stars.
6 An a.... knows about space, but hasn't been there.

Speaking • Review

7 Complete the conversations with these words. 3.10 Then listen and check.

be careful	I were you	~~I wouldn't~~
make sure you	Watch out for	

1 **A** I'm going to swim in the ocean.
   B *I wouldn't* swim alone if .... .
2 **A** I'm going shopping.
   B OK. But .... don't forget your wallet.
3 **A** I'm going for a bike ride.
   B .... the cars. And .... not to stay out after dark.

Dictation

8 Listen and write in your notebook.
3.11

✓ **My assessment profile:** page 144

Science File

Asteroids

● **What are asteroids?**
Asteroids are objects in space that are smaller than planets, and that orbit the sun. They are made of rock or metal, and some have ice on them, too. This is the material that wasn't used when the planets in our solar system were formed 4.5 billion years ago.

● **How many asteroids are there in our solar system?**
Millions. Some are small piles of stones, and these are irregular in shape. But the largest asteroid in our solar system, Ceres, is the shape of a planet and has a diameter of 975 km. That's bigger than France!

● **Where are they?**
There are asteroids in many parts of our solar system, but most of them are in the "asteroid belt" between the orbits of Mars and Jupiter.

● **Do asteroids ever crash into planets?**
Yes, sometimes. In fact, some people think that the moon was created when a huge asteroid crashed into Earth early in our planet's history. Another impact event probably caused the extinction of the dinosaurs and other species about 65 million years ago. These big impact events don't happen very often, but smaller rocks strike Earth about 500 times a year. A lot of big holes in the ground were made by these rocks.

● **Is Earth in danger from asteroids today?**
Sometimes big asteroids pass very close to Earth. In 1989 a 300-meter asteroid passed through the exact position where Earth was only six hours before. If an asteroid of that size hit Earth, there would be an explosion twelve times more powerful than a big nuclear bomb. Astronomers think that about 2,000 asteroids bigger than one kilometer might hit Earth in the next billion years. These will be very dangerous. However, there's nothing terrible to worry about until the year 2880, when a kilometer-wide asteroid has a 1 in 300 chance of hitting Earth.

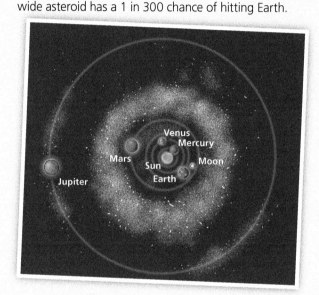

Venus
Mercury
Mars
Sun
Moon
Jupiter
Earth

Reading

 Read the article quickly. What is the size of the biggest asteroid in our solar system?

 Read the article again. Are the statements true (T) or false (F)?
3.12

1 All asteroids are made of rock. *F*
2 Asteroids are many different shapes.
3 Earth's moon used to be an asteroid.
4 An asteroid probably killed the dinosaurs.
5 Rocks from space don't hit Earth very often.
6 A big asteroid will hit Earth in 2880.

Barringer Crater

 Listen to information about the Barringer Crater. Choose the correct options.
3.13

Where?	[1] *the US* / Australia
When?	[2] *5,000 / 50,000* years ago
What?	a piece of [3] *metal / rock*
How big?	[4] *50 / 300* meters
Results?	• a hole in the ground more than [5] *175 m / 1,200 m* wide • all [6] *plants / animals* in a 1,000 km² area were destroyed

My Science File

 Find out about the impact event at either Chicxulub or Tunguska. Make a table about it like the one in Exercise 3.

 Write a short paragraph about the event.

Spies

Vocabulary • Spy collocations

1 Match these phrases to the definitions (1–12). Then listen, check and repeat.

3.14

Grammar
Past perfect;
Third conditional

Vocabulary
Spy collocations;
Adjectives with prefixes
dis-, im-, in-, un-

Speaking
Explaining and
apologizing

Writing
An opinion essay

Word list page 61
Workbook page 131

break into somewhere *9*
decode a message
escape from somewhere
follow someone
make a deal
spy on someone
take cover
tap a phone
tell a lie
tell the truth
track down a person
wear a disguise

1 watch someone secretly
2 find someone after searching for him/her
3 get away from a dangerous place or situation
4 hide in a place to protect yourself
5 discover the meaning of some secret numbers
  or letters
6 use equipment to listen to someone's
  phone calls
7 say the actual facts about something
8 use clothes or other accessories so that
  people can't recognize you
9 get into a place by using force
10 say something untrue
11 agree to do something in exchange for
  something else
12 walk or drive secretly behind a person

2 Look at the picture. Find someone …

taking cover *3*   wearing a disguise
tapping a phone   following another person
making a deal   breaking into somewhere

3 Work in pairs. Have you ever done any of
the things in Exercise 1? Tell your partner.

3.15, 3.16 **Pronunciation Unit 8** page 67

**Brain Trainer Unit 8
Activities 1 and 2**
Go to page 64

Reading

1 **Read the text quickly. Choose the best description.**

1 a newspaper article about spies
2 an extract from a spy novel
3 a biography of a famous spy

2 **Read the text again and answer the questions.**

3.17

1 How did Stella find out where DeVere was?
She decoded a message on her phone.
2 What was Stella probably doing when she
"closed her eyes for a brief moment"?
3 How did Stella get from her apartment
to Hadrian Avenue?
4 Why didn't DeVere need to wear a disguise?
5 How did DeVere get the virus?
6 How did Stella hide from DeVere?
7 Why did she choose this place to hide?
8 Who said, "… in fact I'm right behind *you*"?

3 What about you? **Ask and answer.**

1 How was Stella tricked by DeVere? Can you
find any clues in the text?
2 What do you think happens next?
3 Do you enjoy reading these kinds of stories?
Why?/Why not?

I'M RIGHT BEHIND YOU

The phone call woke her at seven in the morning. There were no words, just a series of strange noises. Stella listened carefully and wrote some numbers on the notepad beside her phone. By the time she put the pen down, she had already decoded the message. It was an address: 22 Hadrian Avenue. Stella opened a street map, moved her finger along the route, closed her eyes for a brief moment, then raced out of her apartment. As she sped through the empty silver streets on her bike, she reviewed what she already knew about her target. Philip DeVere was an ordinary-looking man. Medium height, medium-brown hair, gray-brown eyes. He didn't need to wear a disguise—his face was instantly forgettable. But this unremarkable man was in fact a very dangerous thief. Before he became a criminal, DeVere had been a brilliant scientist. But then two months ago, he broke into the National School of Tropical Medicine and stole a bottle of a deadly virus. Just one drop could pollute the water supply to an entire city. Stella's job was to track down DeVere and get the virus back.

As she approached Hadrian Avenue, Stella jumped off her bike and took cover behind a blue van parked at the corner. From here she had a good view of the street. Number 22 was an old, gray apartment building across from a small, empty children's playground. In the playground there was a woman with a stroller and an old man sitting on a bench reading a newspaper. Suddenly DeVere came running out of number 22 and across the playground.

Stella had already put her cell phone in her pocket before she left her apartment that morning. Now she took it out and dialed a number. "I'm right behind him," she said. She turned off the phone and put it back in her pocket. "Ah, my dear Stella," said a voice, "but in fact I'm right behind *you*!"

Grammar • Past perfect

By the time she put the pen down, she had already decoded the message.

Before he became a criminal, DeVere had been a brilliant scientist.

Stella had already put her cell phone in her pocket before she left her apartment that morning.

Grammar reference page 124

Watch Out!

We often use the following time expressions with the Past perfect:

by the time, by (+ a time), just, already, when

By the time Helen finished her call, she had been on the phone for two hours.

The man had just opened the window when there was a loud explosion.

1 **Study the grammar table and** Watch Out! **Choose the correct options to complete the rules.**

1 We use the Past perfect to describe an action that occurred *before / after* another action in the past.
2 We form the Past perfect with *has / had* + past participle.

2 **Complete the sentences with these words.**

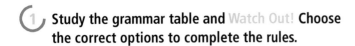

| buy | get | hear | see | ~~send~~ | spend |

1 I lost the letter that you *had sent* the day before.
2 We .... all our money the weekend before, so we couldn't go out last night.
3 He put on the disguise that he .... at the store the day before.
4 We .... just .... home when the phone rang.
5 I .... never .... that song before you sang it last night.
6 She .... never .... a musical before, and she was very excited.

3 **Complete the text with the Past simple or Past perfect form of the verbs.**

By the time Stella ¹ *was* (be) on her way to Hadrian Avenue, DeVere ² .... (already/plan) his escape. He ³ .... (put) on his disguise—a white wig and an old coat. He ⁴ .... (just/pick) up a newspaper when his friend Blaine ⁵ .... (come) to his door. DeVere ⁶ .... (give) Blaine his instructions. "Wait five minutes!" he said. "Then run through the playground to the station." Before Blaine ⁷ .... (have) time to ask any questions, DeVere ⁸ .... (leave) the building. He ⁹ .... (walk) slowly to the park bench and ¹⁰ .... (start) to read his newspaper. After he ¹¹ .... (wait) for five minutes, he ¹² .... (see) Stella turning onto Hadrian Avenue.

4 **Put the sentences into the Past perfect.**

1 I finished my sandwich, and then I ate a banana. (after)
   After I had finished my sandwich, I ate a banana.
2 She opened the window and saw a strange man. (just/when)
3 She put on her coat. Then she left the house. (after)
4 Everyone read the book, and then we discussed it in class. (before).
5 The girl put on her disguise, and then walked into the room. (after)
6 The thief escaped. The alarm bell rang. (already, by the time)

5 **Use the Past perfect to make endings to the sentences.**

1 When I arrived at the theater *the movie had already started.*
2 When I opened the door …
3 Julie felt sad because …
4 There was no school yesterday because …
5 I was really happy because …

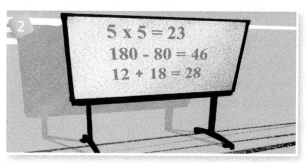

Vocabulary • Adjectives with prefixes
dis-, im-, in-, un-

1 **Match the pictures (1–4) to these adjectives.**

> dishonest   impossible *1*   incorrect   unfair

2 **Copy the table. Put the words under the correct headings. Then listen, check your answers and repeat.**

3.18

> | appropriate | ~~correct~~ | ~~fair~~ | ~~honest~~ |
> | important | loyal | patient | polite |
> | ~~possible~~ | satisfied | successful | tolerant |

dis-	im-	in-	un-
dishonest	*impossible*	*incorrect*	*unfair*
....	....	....	....
....	....	....	....

Word list page 61
Workbook page 131

3 **Complete the sentences with words from Exercise 2.**

1 Our team didn't win the game. We were *unsuccessful*.
2 He said he was sorry, but she was .... with his apology and didn't reply to his letter.
3 This answer is .... . Please look at it again.
4 If you don't support your friends when they have problems, people might think you are .... .
5 This movie is very violent. It's .... for children.
6 My sister never says "please" or "thank you." She's really .... !
7 My dad's boss is very ....—he doesn't like people to disagree with him.
8 You can't get from London to New York in one hour. It's .... !
9 The .... boy cheated on his math exam.
10 I know you think this problem is .... , but it's really worrying me.
11 My sister's piece of cake is much bigger than mine. It's so .... !
12 She's never prepared to wait for other people—she's really .... .

4 **What about you? In pairs, tell your partner about**

1 a time when you were honest.
2 a time when you felt something was unfair.
3 two situations that make you feel impatient.

> **Brain Trainer Unit 8**
> **Activity 3**
> Go to page 64

Speaking and Listening

1 **Look at the photo. What is Archie's dad doing? Is Archie happy or angry about this?**

2 **Listen and read the conversation.**
3.19 **Check your answers.**

3 **Listen and read again. Answer the questions.**
3.19
1 Why is Archie's dad looking at Archie's computer?
He wants to check who Archie is talking to online.
2 Does Archie understand that he should be careful about online safety?
3 Why does Archie's dad worry about Archie's online friends?
4 Why does Archie think that this social networking site is safe?
5 Why is Archie so angry with his dad?

4 **Act out the conversation in pairs.**

Archie	What's going on, Dad? Why are you using my computer?
Dad	I'm checking your social networking account.
Archie	That's uncalled for! You're spying on my private conversations. It's totally unfair.
Dad	No, Archie, that's not true. But the fact is that you have to be careful about who you talk to online.
Archie	I know that! I would have told you immediately if a stranger had ever tried to contact me online. But nothing like that has ever happened.
Dad	I'm sure that's true. But you have to understand that some people can be dishonest about their real identity.
Archie	I'm aware of that, Dad. But there's nothing inappropriate on this social networking site. It's approved by my school.
Dad	Well, let's forget about it, OK? I'm sorry that I upset you.
Archie	OK, whatever. But if you had asked me first, I wouldn't have gotten so angry.

Say it in your language ...
What's going on?
That's uncalled for!

Look at the conversation again. Who says what?

1 It's totally unfair. *Archie*
2 The fact is that …
3 I know that!
4 I'm sure that's true.
5 You have to understand that …
6 Let's forget about it.

 Read the phrases for explaining, acknowledging and apologizing.

Explaining, acknowledging and apologizing	
Explaining	The fact is that … You have to understand that …
Acknowledging	I know that. I'm aware of that. I'm sure that's true.
Apologizing and accepting an apology	I'm sorry that … Let's forget about it.

 Listen to the conversation. Act out the conversation in pairs.

3.20

Holly Yasmin, why are you ¹ using my phone?
Yasmin ² I'm looking for Fraser's number.
Holly Well, you should ask me first. ³ My phone is private.
Yasmin The fact is that you weren't here, and ⁴ I need his number now.
Holly I'm sure that's true. But you shouldn't look at other people's stuff without asking.
Yasmin OK, I'm sorry that I upset you.

 Work in pairs. Replace the words in purple in Exercise 7. Use these phrases and/or your own ideas. Act out the conversations.

1 read my diary / in my bedroom / look at my email account

2 want to check when Mark's birthday is / try to find my jacket / look for Sara's email address

3 my diary / my bedroom / my email account

4 organize his party / need my jacket now / want to send her this photo now

Grammar • Third conditional

If you had asked me first, I wouldn't have gotten so angry.
(You didn't ask me first, so I was angry.)

I would have told you immediately if a stranger had tried to contact me.
(A stranger didn't try to contact me, so I didn't tell you.)

Grammar reference page 124

 Study the grammar table. Choose the correct options to complete the rules.

1 We use the Third conditional to talk about *unreal / real* situations in the past.
2 We form the Third conditional with *if + Past perfect / Past participle + would(n't) have + Past perfect / Past participle*.

 Which are the Third conditional (3) sentences?

1 If I hadn't taken the bus, I would have walked home. *3*
2 If I met Lady Gaga, I would ask for her autograph. ….
3 You wouldn't have failed the test if you had worked harder. ….
4 She would buy a new car if she won $10,000.

 Complete the sentences with the correct form of the verbs. Use the Third conditional.

1 If we *had known* (know) about your party, we *would have gone* (go) to it.
2 If it …. (not rain) yesterday, we …. (play) tennis.
3 If you …. (watch) that horror movie, you …. (be) very scared!
4 Marie …. (practice) the violin this morning if she …. (not hurt) her arm.
5 I …. (help) you if I …. (be) there.

 What about you? **Write answers to these questions. Use the Third conditional.**

1 Why were you so late yesterday?
   I missed the bus. If I hadn't missed the bus, I wouldn't have been late.
2 Why didn't you go to school yesterday?
3 Why did you yell at your friend last night?
4 Why didn't you go swimming last weekend?

Who's Watching You?

Ted Barnes is a typical 16-year-old student at a large high school in Pittsburgh. He walks to school every morning, attends classes, eats his lunch in the school cafeteria, takes out books from the school library and sometimes goes to an after-school computer club before he walks home. And like most of his classmates, Ted is under surveillance throughout his school day. On his way to school, he walks past four CCTV cameras. Ted's school has thirty CCTV cameras in the hallways and near the school entrance. When Ted checks out books from his library, he uses a fingerprint scanner, and when he buys his lunch in the cafeteria, he uses an ID card, which records what he buys. After school, at computer club, the teacher can see exactly which sites Ted visits and can monitor his online conversations. Ted and many of his friends feel more and more dissatisfied with the level of surveillance in their lives. "Teachers, the police, our parents … they're spying on us all the time. They think that our right to privacy is unimportant," complains Ted. "They don't tap our phones, but they follow us in so many other ways. Nothing is private anymore."

But Andrew Lott, the principal at Ted's school, argues that surveillance is a useful and necessary part of school life. "Before we installed cameras here, students had reported a lot of problems with bullying. We had tried to identify the bullies, but before the CCTV cameras, we were unsuccessful. After we had installed the cameras, we identified the bullies and noticed an immediate improvement in discipline. Now our students know that they are safe at school. If we hadn't put cameras in the hallways, we wouldn't have been able to track down the bullies. It's impossible to have a system that makes everyone happy."

Key Words

surveillance	check out
fingerprint scanner	monitor
privacy	install

Reading

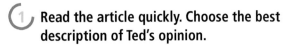

1 Read the article quickly. Choose the best description of Ted's opinion.

1 There is too much surveillance in our daily lives.
2 Surveillance is important to keep us safe.
3 We need to find better ways than surveillance to protect students.

2 Read the article again. Are these statements true (T), false (F) or don't know (DK)?
3.21

1 Ted is like most other 16-year-old students. *T*
2 Ted goes home at the same time every day.
3 Ted's school can find out what he eats for lunch.
4 There are CCTV cameras in the computer club classroom.
5 Ted thinks that some people are listening to his phone conversations.
6 Andrew Lott agrees with Ted that there is too much surveillance at school.
7 Before CCTV cameras were installed, bullying was the biggest problem at the school.

Listening

1 Listen to the interview. How many students does the reporter talk to? Do they agree with each other?
3.22

 Listening Bank Unit 8 page 66

2 Discuss the questions.

1 Do you have CCTV cameras at your school? If so, where are they?
2 Do you think that CCTV cameras can help stop problems like bullying and theft at school?
3 Do you think that CCTV cameras are an invasion of your privacy?

Writing • An opinion essay

 Read the Writing File.

Writing File Expressing opinions

Introductory paragraph

• **State the topic of the essay and your main opinion.**

Our local council is planning to close the gym and open a new swimming pool. In my opinion,/I think this is an excellent idea.

Middle paragraphs

• **Give reasons for your opinion. Use a new paragraph for each reason.**

In the first place/First, I feel that …
I'm also convinced/I also believe that …
Another point to bear in mind is …
Finally, …

Conclusion

• **State your main opinion again, and give a brief summary of the reasons.**

To conclude, I believe that … because …
In conclusion, my view is that …

 Put the parts of an essay (a–e) in the correct order.

a In the first place, many parents have already spent a lot of money on the current school uniform this year.

b In conclusion, I am against the introduction of a new school uniform because it will be both more expensive and unpopular.

c Our school wants to introduce a new school uniform. In my opinion, this is a bad idea. *1*

d Finally, the suggested new uniform is much more expensive, and this will affect parents with several children at the school.

e I also believe that our current uniform is very dressy and popular, and most students are proud of it.

 Read the essay and find the language from the Writing File.

Our school has announced plans to introduce fingerprint scanning in the library. I think this is a really good idea.

In the first place, while it's easy to lose or forget a library card or a PIN, you can't lose your fingers! So students can always take out books when they need to.

I also believe that people can't steal or duplicate fingerprints. Students therefore don't need to worry about other people taking out books in their name.

Although some opponents of the plan think that fingerprint scanning is an invasion of privacy, I'm convinced that they are wrong. The school doesn't store the fingerprints. It converts each fingerprint into a code so no one can steal it or use it.

In conclusion, I believe that fingerprint scanning is a more secure way of borrowing books from the library, and it doesn't threaten students' privacy.

 Read the essay again and answer the questions.

1 Is the writer for or against fingerprint scanning? *for*
2 How many reasons does the writer give for his/her opinion?
3 What are the advantages of fingerprint scanning?
4 Why does the writer think that fingerprint scanning won't threaten students' privacy?

 You are going to write an opinion essay. Read the text below. Use ideas from page 44.

Your school is planning to install 45 CCTV cameras in the hallways and classrooms.
• Decide whether you are for or against the plan.
• Plan your paragraphs.
• Include at least three reasons to support your opinion.

 Now write your opinion essay. Use your ideas from Exercise 5.

Remember!
• Use clear paragraphs and language for giving your opinion.
• Use the vocabulary in this unit.
• Check your grammar, spelling and punctuation.

Refresh Your Memory!

Grammar • Review

 1 **Complete the sentences with the Past simple or Past perfect form of the verbs.**

1 We *had already eaten* (already/eat) lunch before we *went* (go) to the café.
2 By the time I .... (get) to school, the class .... (start).
3 When I .... (arrive) at the movie theater, I .... (see) a long line of people. Some of them .... (be) there for hours, and others .... (just/arrive).
4 I .... (meet) James two years before, but I .... (not/recognize) him when he .... (speak) to me.
5 After she .... (finish) her homework, she .... (watch) TV.
6 We .... (just/open) the window when a bird .... (fly) into the room.

2 **Match the beginnings (1–5) to the endings (a–e) of the sentences.**

1 If she hadn't pulled the dog's tail, *d*
2 If I hadn't lost my phone,
3 If you had remembered your umbrella,
4 If we had been kinder to her,
5 If you had asked me first,

a I would have called you.
b I would have said yes.
c you wouldn't have gotten so wet.
d it wouldn't have bitten her.
e she wouldn't have been so upset.

 3 **Make sentences. Use the Third conditional.**

1 I didn't remember my books. The librarian was angry.
   If I had remembered my books, the librarian wouldn't have been angry.
2 They woke up late. They missed their favorite show on TV.
3 We didn't study for the test. We didn't pass it.
4 She ate a lot of chocolate. She felt sick.
5 Fred and his sister visited their aunt. They didn't go to the football game.
6 I fell asleep during the movie. I didn't understand the ending.

Vocabulary • Review

 4 **Complete the sentences with the correct form of these words.**

break	decode	escape	follow	make	~~spy~~
take	tap	tell (x2)	track	wear	

1 Someone is *spying* on me! A man .... me home yesterday, and I think someone has .... our phone!
2 Can you .... this strange message?
3 OK, I'll .... a deal with you. If you tell me who .... into the school last weekend, I'll give you $50.
4 The police have .... down the dangerous criminal, Harry Thug, who .... from prison last night.
5 Look! It's Tim! He's .... a disguise!
6 Most people don't always .... the truth.
7 I quickly .... cover behind the tree.
8 That girl's .... a lie! I saw her cheat on the exam!

 5 **Use the prefixes dis-, im-, in- or un- to complete the adjectives.**

1 *in*appropriate
2 ....correct
3 ....fair
4 ....patient
5 ....important
6 ....honest
7 ....polite
8 ....loyal
9 ...satisfied
10 ...successful

Speaking • Review

 6 **Put the conversation in the correct order.**
3.23 **Then listen and check.**

a I know that. But the fact is that I left my wallet on your desk this morning. So maybe you put it in your bag. I'm sorry that I upset you.
b What are you doing with my bag? *1*
c It's not in my bag! And you have to understand that it's important to ask before taking someone's bag.
d OK. Let's forget about it.
e I'm looking for my wallet.

Dictation

 7 **Listen and write in your notebook.**
3.24

My assessment profile: page 145

Marnie Higgins's Profile*

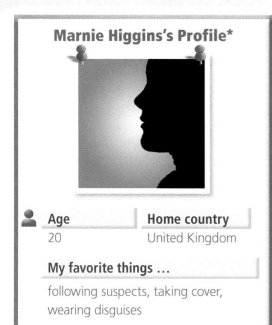

Age	Home country
20	United Kingdom

My favorite things …

following suspects, taking cover, wearing disguises

Reading

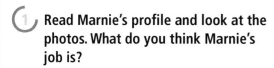

1 Read Marnie's profile and look at the photos. What do you think Marnie's job is?

2 Read the text. Answer the questions.

3.25

1 According to the author, what is the typical image of a private detective?
A middle-aged man wearing a brown coat and a fedora hat.

2 Where does Marnie work?

3 What did Marnie do when she first started working there?

4 Why does Marnie think that young people are better at surveillance?

5 Is the job always dangerous?

6 Why was Marnie's car full of sandwich boxes and magazines?

7 How does Marnie's boss make sure that she is always safe?

8 What does Marnie do now?

*Her photo can't be shown because of her job.

FOLLOW THAT CAR!

When we think of private detectives, we usually imagine middle-aged men dressed in brown coats and wearing fedora hats. But a successful detective agency in southeastern England has a special group of "teen detectives." One of these detectives is Marnie, who started working for the agency while she was still in school. Her first job wasn't as a detective—she was a data entry clerk, but "it was more exciting than stacking shelves in a supermarket!" Marnie explains. One day, one of the other detectives was following a suspect, and he asked Marnie to pretend to be his niece. "I was scared, but it was also really thrilling!" Marnie is now 20 years old, but sometimes she wears a disguise and pretends to be a high school student. "Young people are better at surveillance," she explains. "If you notice a student standing on a street corner, you probably won't suspect she's a private detective!"

But isn't the job very dangerous? "Sometimes it is, but often it's just very boring. When you do surveillance work, you often have to wait in one place for hours and hours. Last week I was in my car outside someone's house for six hours. By the time I had finished, the car was full of magazines, and empty sandwich boxes and soft-drink cans!" Marnie's boss, the head of the detective agency, is careful to protect her safety. "My detectives always wear a 'bug'—a hidden microphone—so that I can follow them and listen to them. If the situation gets dangerous, we step in very quickly." Marnie now combines her detective work with college studies. "Many of the undergraduates in my major have part-time jobs while they study, but I'm the only private detective!"

Class discussion

1 Would you like Marnie's job? Why?/Why not?

2 What would your parents say if you got a job with a detective agency?

3 What personal qualities do you think a private detective needs? Make a list.

9 Celebrate!

Grammar
Reported statements, commands and requests, questions

Vocabulary
Party collocations;
Reporting verbs

Speaking
Reaching an agreement

Writing
A problem page

Word list page 61
Workbook page 132

Vocabulary • Party collocations

1 Complete the phrases (1–13) with these words. Then listen, check and repeat.

3.26

do
go
greet
have
hire
make
put up
stay up
~~throw~~
wear (x4)

1 *throw* a party
2 .... a jacket and tie
3 .... dressy clothes
4 .... your hair
5 .... high heels
6 .... decorations
7 .... a DJ
8 .... by limo
9 .... casual clothes
10 .... the time of your life
11 .... all night
12 .... your guests
13 .... a speech

2 Complete the text with words from Exercise 1.

Every year on Oscar night, the world's most famous movie stars ¹ *go* by ² *limo* to the Oscars ceremony in Hollywood. No one wears ³ .... that night. The men wear a ⁴ .... and ⁵.... . The women wear ⁶ .... clothes too, usually a beautiful long dress and ⁷.... on their feet. A professional has done their ⁸ .... . At the ceremony, each Oscar winner has to ⁹.... a ¹⁰ .... to say "thank you." Then, after the ceremony, some celebrities ¹¹ .... a ¹² .... for their friends. They ¹³ .... their ¹⁴ .... and give them champagne and expensive food. A lot of people ¹⁵ .... all ¹⁶ .... . No one wants to go to bed when they're having the ¹⁷ .... their ¹⁸ .... .

3 Describe the photos on this page. Use words from Exercise 1.

In picture a, they've hired a DJ. Everyone's wearing ...

4 In pairs, ask and answer the questions.

Do you, your family or your friends ever throw parties? What do you do to get ready for them? What do you do at them? What do you wear?

🎧 3.27, 3.28 **Pronunciation Unit 9** page 67

Brain Trainer Unit 9
Activities 1 and 2
Go to page 64

Reading

1 Look at the photos and the title.
Answer the questions.

1 What are proms?
2 Who goes to them?
3 Which country has them?
4 Is it expensive to go to a prom?

2 Read the article and check your answers
to Exercise 1.

3 Read the article again and answer the questions.

3.29
1 What transportation do people use to get to
the prom? *They go by limo.*
2 What, according to the article, is wrong with
students' ideas for proms?
3 What do people have to pay for if they want
to go to a prom?
4 Which teenagers liked the proms at the New
View School?
5 Why did some students get weekend jobs?
6 Why were these jobs a problem?
7 What differences are there between
the graduation party and a prom?

4 What about you? In pairs, ask and answer.

1 Does your school throw a party for its seniors?
What kind of party?
2 Would you like to go to a prom? Why?/Why not?
3 How much money should people spend on a
party like a prom? How much is too much?

Prom Night

A prom is a special party for high school seniors, and it's an important tradition in the US. The girls wear a beautiful dress; the boys wear a special evening suit called a tuxedo. They go to the party by limo, which for many is the highlight of their school career.

The average 18-year-old now spends $1,139 on his or her prom night, up from $1,098 last year and $807 the year before. There are the costs of prom tickets, clothes and a limo, and the girls often ask professionals to do their hair, nails and makeup.

Additionally, students always want their prom to be better than the one held the year before. It becomes a kind of competition, and some schools are not happy about this.

"Our school used to have proms in a hotel," says Mr. Turner, principal of the New View School in Phoenix, Arizona. "The richer kids loved them. But others told me they couldn't afford to go. Teachers said that some kids had found weekend jobs to pay for the prom and, as a result, weren't doing enough school work. Finally, we told the students that there wouldn't be any more proms."

Were they disappointed? "Some were, of course. But this year we threw a graduation party in the school auditorium. We told the kids to put up cheap decorations and bring their own music. They wore casual clothes. Everyone felt relaxed, and the kids had the time of their lives."

Grammar • Reported statements

Present simple → Past simple

"Your dress is nice."
→ They said that my dress was nice.

Present continuous → Past continuous

"They aren't doing enough work."
→ He told me that they weren't doing enough work.

Past simple → Past perfect

"The richer kids loved the prom."
→ He told the journalist that the richer kids had loved the prom.

Present perfect → Past perfect

"We have found weekend jobs."
→ They said that they had found weekend jobs.

Grammar reference page 126

will → would

"There won't be a prom."
→ We told them that there wouldn't be a prom.

am/is/are going to → was/were going to

"We're going to be there."
→ They told us that they were going to be there.

have to/must → had to

"I must buy a new jacket."
→ He said that he had to buy a new jacket.

can → could

"I can't afford a new car."
→ He told me that he couldn't afford a new car."

1 Study the grammar table. Choose the correct options to complete the rules.

> 1 When we report a statement with *said* or *told*, the tense goes *forward / back* in time.
> 2 There is *always / never* an object after *said*.
> 3 There is *always / never* an object after *told*.

Watch Out!

In reported speech, pronouns and place and time expressions sometimes have to change.
For example:
now → then
here → there
this week → that week
last month → the month before
next year → the following year

2 Complete the sentences. Use reported speech.

1 "It's a great party."
→ He said that it *was* a great party.
2 "I talked to some nice people."
→ He told me that he .... to some nice people.
3 "I really like Lara."
→ He said that he really .... Lara.
4 "I must see her again."
→ He said that he .... her again.
5 "I've sent her a text message."
→ He told me that he .... her a text message.
6 "I can meet you later."
→ Lara told him that she .... him later.
7 "I'll wait for you at the park."
→ He told Lara that he .... for her at the park.
8 "We're going to go to the movies."
→ He said that they .... to the movies.

3 Read the conversation. Then complete the text below. Use reported speech.

Mia The Fourth of July fireworks are next Tuesday.
Otto I can't think about the Fourth of July now. I'm too busy this week.
Mia You weren't here for July 4 last year. We have to go together this year. It'll be fun.

Mia told Otto that the Fourth of July fireworks were [1] *the following Tuesday.* Otto said that [2] .... couldn't think about the Fourth of July [3] .... because he was too busy [4] .... . Mia said that [5] .... hadn't been [6] .... for July 4 [7] .... . She told him that [8] .... had to go together [9] .... . She said that it [10] .... be fun.

• Reported commands and requests

"Put up decorations."
→ I told you to put up decorations.

"Can you do our hair, please?"/"Please do our hair."
→ They asked her to do their hair.

"Don't hire a DJ."
→ He told us not to hire a DJ.

Grammar reference page 126

1 Study the grammar box. Choose the correct options.

> 1 When we are reporting a command or request,
>   we use the *infinitive / -ing* form.
> 2 In the negative, we use *don't / not* + infinitive.
> 3 We *use / don't use* "please" in reported requests.

2 Make commands and requests. Use reported speech.

1 "Please eat some food." (He asked us …)
  He asked us to eat some food.
2 "Don't cancel the party." (She told him …)
3 "Don't worry about the noise." (They told her …)
4 "Could you help with the decorations?"
  (She asked me …)
5 "Don't wear casual clothes." (They told us …)

3 Work in pairs. Give your partner a command. Your partner does the action and reports what you have said.

> Touch your ear with your hand!

4 Make sentences. Use commands, requests or statements in reported speech.

1 "We're going to cook sausages tonight."
  → They told her *that they were going to cook sausages that night.*
2 "Don't forget the bread."
  → I told him …
3 "I've always loved watching fireworks."
  → She said …
4 "Please come to my Halloween party."
  → She asked me …
5 "It'll be fun."
  → She told me …

Vocabulary • Reporting verbs

1 Match the verbs in bold in the sentences (1–10) to
3.30 the definitions (a–j). Then listen, check and repeat.

1 She **admitted** that she'd broken my laptop. *d*
2 He **agreed** to do the vacuuming.
3 They **complained** that the music was terrible.
4 She **explained** that a "paw paw" is a type of fruit.
5 We **invited** him to go on vacation with us.
6 He **mentioned** that he had seen you at the party.
7 She **offered** to bring some food. She's so kind.
8 We **promised** to take care of him.
9 I **refused** to help him. He can do it himself.
10 He **warned** us not to make a mess.

a give information so someone can understand it
b tell someone that you will definitely do something
c talk about something during a conversation
d agree that something is true
e ask someone to come to an event with you
f say that you won't do something
g say yes to an idea or plan
h say that you are happy to do something helpful
i tell someone that something bad might happen
j say that you are annoyed about something

Word list page 61   **Workbook** page 132

2 Which pattern do the verbs in Exercise 1 follow? What about *say, tell* and *ask*?

1 verb + object (+ *not*) + infinitive *invite*, …
2 verb (+ *not*) + infinitive
3 verb + *that* + reported statement

3 Complete the sentences. Use the structures from Exercise 2.

1 "I'm not going to do it." He refused *to do it.*
2 "My leg hurts." She complained …. .
3 "Have dinner with me, Lulu." He invited …. .
4 "Don't be late, children." She warned …. .
5 "OK, I'll write to her." I agreed …. .
6 "I forgot about the party." She admitted …. .
7 "It's my birthday soon." He mentioned …. .
8 "We'll carry the boxes." They offered …. .
9 "I can't afford the ticket." She explained …. .
10 "I won't tell anyone." She promised …. .

> **Brain Trainer Unit 9**
> **Activity 3**
> Go to page 64

Speaking and Listening

1 Look at the photo. Answer the questions.

   1 What are the friends wearing?
   2 Where are they going?
   3 Why are they riding bikes?

2 Listen and read the conversation.
3.31 Check your answers.

3 Listen and read again. Answer the questions.
3.31
   1 Who booked the limo? *Archie*
   2 Why does Archie make a phone call?
   3 Why hasn't the limo driver arrived yet?
   4 When is he going to arrive?
   5 Why doesn't Yasmin want to walk to school?
   6 Why do they decide to go by bike?

4 Act out the conversation in groups of four.

Yasmin	Hey, Archie, what color is our limo for the prom?
Archie	I don't know. I asked how much it was, but I didn't ask about the color. The driver agreed to be here by seven. What time is it now?
Fraser	Seven fifteen. Why don't we call him?
Archie	That's a good idea. I'll go and call now. (*Later*) Oh man. I asked him if he was almost here, and he admitted that he'd forgotten all about us!
Holly	Is he coming now?
Archie	No, he said he couldn't come.
Yasmin	But that's a disaster!
Fraser	It's not the end of the world. Do you think we could walk to school?
Yasmin	No way! I'm wearing high heels.
Holly	Then I think we should go by bike. We can get to school pretty quickly that way.
Archie	That makes sense. Come on, everyone!

Say it in your language ...
That's a disaster!
It's not the end of the world.

5 Look back at the conversation. Who says what?

1 Why don't we call him? *Fraser*
2 That's a good idea.
3 Do you think we could walk to school?
4 No way!
5 I think we should go by bike.
6 That makes sense.

6 Read the phrases for reaching an agreement.

Making suggestions
Do you think we could …?
I think we should …
Maybe we can …
Why don't we …?

Agreeing	Disagreeing
That's a good idea.	I don't think we should …
That makes sense.	No way!

7 Listen to the conversations. What do the speakers agree to do? Act out the conversations.

3.32

Yasmin ¹ We've run out of food.
Holly Why don't we ² walk to the store?
Yasmin No way! ³ It's raining.
Holly Do you think we could ⁴ ask Archie to get some chips from his house?
Yasmin That's a good idea. Let's do that.

Archie ¹ There aren't any tickets for Saturday.
Fraser Maybe we can ² go on Sunday.
Archie I don't think we should do that. ³ It'll end late, and we'll have school the next day.
Fraser Then I think we should ⁴ go on Friday.
Archie That makes sense. OK.

8 Work in pairs. Replace the words in purple in Exercise 7. Use these words and/or your own ideas. Act out the conversations.

1 It's her birthday tomorrow. / The buses are canceled. / We need a DJ for the party.

2 throw her a party / go by bike / hire someone

3 It's too late. / It's too far. / DJs are expensive.

4 make her a birthday card / ask your mom to drive us / ask my brother to be the DJ

Grammar • Reported questions

Wh questions
"How much is it?" → I asked how much it was.
"Where were you?" → She asked me where I'd been.

yes/no questions
"Do you like my dress?" → She asked him if he liked her dress.
"Will they bike to the party?" → We asked if they would bike to the party.

Grammar reference page 126

1 Study the grammar table. Choose the correct options to complete the rules.

1 The word order in reported questions is the same as in an ordinary *question / statement*.
2 We *use / don't use do, does* and *did*.
3 The tense in the reported question *changes / doesn't change*.
4 We introduce a *yes/no* reported question with *if / that*.

2 Make the questions into reported questions.

1 "Where are you going, Mike?" asked Suzie.
   Suzie asked Mike where he was going.
2 "Kate, have you seen Millie?" I asked.
3 "What did you wear to the prom?" she asked me.
4 "Ben, will you be in Seattle tomorrow?" they asked.

3 Read the conversation. Then complete the text below. Use reported questions.

Dan Hey, Joy! Great party! Who's the girl with short dark hair?
Joy She's my friend Ella's sister.
Dan Does she go to our school?
Joy No, she goes to school in San Francisco.
Dan Uh … Does she have a boyfriend?
Joy I don't know.
Dan Can you please find out for me?

Dan asked Joy ¹ *who the girl with short dark hair was*, and Joy told him ² …. . Dan asked her ³ …. , and Joy said ⁴ …. . After that, he asked Joy ⁵ …. . When Joy said ⁶ …. , Dan asked her ⁷ …. for him.

Reading ⌒

1 Look at the title and the photos. What is happening in each one? Match three of the photos to the countries (1–3).

1 Taiwan
2 Mexico
3 Brazil

Coming of Age

We asked young people around the world what made them an adult in their country. Here are some of the most fascinating answers that we received.

Huang | Taiwan

In my country, we have a special ceremony for all sixteen-year-olds. I did the ceremony last year. Before it, my mother explained the traditions. She said that the goddess Chiniangma had taken care of me for the first sixteen years of my life, but now I had to share the adult responsibilities in the family. At the beginning of the ceremony, I had to wash my hands in a special bowl, as a sign that I was washing away my old habits. Then I had to crawl under a wooden pagoda that my parents were holding. This was my journey into adult life.

Nerea | Mexico

Girls in Mexico become adults on their fifteenth birthday. Their parents throw a big party called *quince años*. First, you go to church, and after that, all the guests meet in a hotel. Traditionally, this party is the first time that a Mexican girl dances in public, and the first time that she puts on makeup. In the middle of the party, the girl's father takes off her flat shoes and puts high heels on her feet, as a sign that she's now a woman.

Bruno | Brazil

As in Mexico, girls in Brazil have a big party when they are fifteen. But some tribes in the Brazilian rain forest have much scarier traditions. The boys of the Satere-Mawe tribe have to put their hands into gloves full of poisonous ants for ten minutes. I saw a TV show about it, and it said that each ant sting hurt thirty times more than a wasp sting. The boys have to do this glove ceremony twenty times to become an adult!

Key Words

ceremony	crawl	pagoda
flat	ants	sting
wasp		

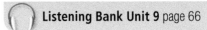

2 Read the article quickly and check your ideas.

3 Read the article again. Which country has
3.33 coming-of-age ceremonies …

1 for   a) girls? *Mexico*   b) boys and girls?
2 for people age   a) fifteen?   b) sixteen?
3 that involve   a) water?   b) animals?

4 Read the article again. Answer the questions.
3.33
1 How did Huang learn about the meaning of his ceremony? *from his mother*
2 What was the meaning of his crawl under the wooden pagoda?
3 According to Mexican tradition, what two things shouldn't girls do before they are fifteen?
4 What change happens during a *quince años* party?
5 Where does the Satere-Mawe tribe live?
6 Why is the glove ceremony scary?

Listening ⌒

1 Look at photo c and listen to a radio interview.
3.34 Answer the questions.

1 What country is this?
2 How old are the girls in the photo?
3 What have they done today?

🎧 **Listening Bank Unit 9** page 66

2 What about you? Ask and answer the questions in pairs.

1 How old are people in your country when they become adults? Do you think it is the right age?
2 Are there any coming-of-age traditions in your country? Describe them.
3 What do you think of the ceremonies in the pictures? Which of them would you like to experience, and which not? Why?

Writing • A problem page

1 Read the Writing File.

Writing File Referencing

Try not to repeat the same nouns too often in your writing. Use pronouns and possessive adjectives instead.

- I like parties. ~~Parties~~ They *are fun.*
- *It's Mark's birthday. I'm giving* ~~Mark~~ him *a T-shirt.*
- *Lia's dress is nice, and* ~~Lia's~~ her *shoes are cool, too.*

2 Read part of a problem page in a magazine. What nouns do the underlined words replace?

Problem Page

Dear Amy,

It's my birthday next week and I've asked four of my friends to go out for dinner with me. Last week ¹ <u>they</u> *my friends* all said that they could go, but this morning three of ² <u>them</u> told me that they had made other plans. I'm really upset. Should I cancel my birthday dinner, or have ³ <u>it</u> with the one friend who is still free?

Matt

Dear Matt,

I'm sorry to hear about your problem. It is often hard to organize parties and birthday celebrations!

Did you ask your friends why they had changed ⁴ <u>their</u> plans? They probably had a good reason. For example, maybe your dinner finishes late on a school night, and their parents told them that ⁵ <u>they</u> couldn't go to ⁶ <u>it</u>. Or maybe they had already promised to do something else before you invited them, but they had forgotten about ⁷ <u>it</u>. If their reason is good enough, you should arrange your dinner for a night that is easier for everyone. However, it's possible that these people don't really want to be at your dinner. If that is true, you should have ⁸ <u>it</u> without ⁹ <u>them</u>. One real friend is better than a group of false friends, in my opinion.

Good luck. I hope you have the time of your life on your birthday. Relax and enjoy ¹⁰ <u>it</u>!

Amy

3 Read Amy's answer again and answer the questions.

1 How does she feel about the problem?
2 What three possible reasons for the problem does she mention?
3 What two solutions does she suggest?
4 What final advice does she give?

4 Read the problem. What do you think the solution is?

Dear Amy,

Last week my mom said that I could have a birthday party at my house, but now she's changed her mind. The problem is that I've already invited all my friends. What should I do? It'll be terrible if I cancel the party.

Charlotte

5 Match the reasons (1–5) to the solutions (a–e).

1 Mom is worried about the noise. e
2 Mom is too busy.
3 Mom is worried about the mess.
4 Mom thinks you're not reliable enough.
5 Mom thinks you'll stay up all night.

a Change the date of the party.
b Have the party in the backyard or at a park.
c Promise to end the party early.
d Say that there won't be any bad behavior.
e Promise not to play loud music.

6 Write a reply to the problem. Use the questions in Exercise 3, the ideas from Exercise 5 and the outline below to help you.

Paragraph 1
Express sympathy with the writer.
Paragraph 2
Discuss some reasons for the problem and some possible solutions.
Paragraph 3
End with some positive words and some final advice.

Remember!
- Use pronouns and possessive adjectives so you don't repeat nouns too often.
- Use vocabulary and grammar from this unit.
- Check your grammar, spelling and punctuation.

Refresh Your Memory!

Grammar • Review

1 **Make sentences. Use reported speech.**

1 "I am from Venice, Italy." (She said …)
   She said she was from Venice, Italy.
2 "I loved the carnival last year." (She told me …)
3 "I've never seen such great fireworks." (She said …)
4 "I'll send you some photos." (She told me …)
5 "We're going to invite a lot of friends next year." (She said …)
6 I hope you can come, too." (She told me …)

2 **Complete the text with the correct form of these verbs.**

buy	cook	go	not complain
not give	play	ride	

In the morning, Mom asked me ¹ *to buy* some pizzas on the way home from school. But after school, my friend asked me ² …. soccer with him, and I forgot about the pizzas. When I got home, Mom asked me ³ …. my bike to the store, but I told her ⁴ …. me all the jobs. She got angry and told me ⁵ …. to my room. Later, I said that I was hungry and asked her ⁶ …. something, but she told me ⁷ …. . It's nine o'clock, and I haven't eaten anything since lunch!

3 **Make reported questions.**

1 "When are the guests arriving?" he asked.
   He asked when the guests were arriving.
2 "Why did Sam get here late?" he asked.
3 "Did he bring any food?" we asked.
4 "Do I have to wear a tie?" he asked.
5 "Can I choose the music?" she asked.
6 "What time are we going to leave?" I asked.

4 **Put the text into reported speech.**

"Where are you, Sophie?" asked Connor.
Connor asked Sophie where she was.
"Hurry up!" he told her. "The prom is starting soon."
"I haven't done my hair," said Sophie. Then she asked, "Are my high heels in the hall?"
Connor looked. "They aren't here," he said, "and it's already six fifteen."
"Go without me," said Sophie. "I'll come later."
"Don't worry," said Connor. "I'm happy to wait."

Vocabulary • Review

5 **Complete the text with these words.**

all night	casual clothes	decorations
DJ	dressy clothes	hair
high heels	jacket and tie	limo
~~party~~	time of our lives	

My friends and I are going to throw a ¹ *party* this July. We've hired a ² …. for the music, and we're going to put up a lot of ³ …. . Everyone's going to wear ⁴ …. : a ⁵ …. for the boys, and a dress and ⁶ …. for the girls. If anyone wears ⁷ …. , they won't be allowed into the party. My friends and I are going to do our ⁸ …. at my house. We're going to go to the party by ⁹ …. . We're planning to stay up ¹⁰ …. , and I'm sure we'll have the ¹¹ …. .

6 **Complete the sentences with these verbs.**

admitted	complained	offered
promised	~~refused~~	warned

1 He was tired, so he *refused* to go running with us.
2 We …. that the school food tasted awful.
3 They …. to come, so why aren't they here?
4 I …. you not to touch that dog. It bites.
5 She …. that she had cheated on the exam.
6 I …. to help her, but she didn't want any help.

Speaking • Review

7 **Put the conversation in the correct order.**
3.35 **Then listen and check.**

a That makes sense. Who can we ask?
b Why don't we go to the store and buy some more?
c We don't have enough decorations. *1*
d I think we should ask Katie. Her parents have a lot of useful things in their attic.
e That's a good idea. Let's go to her house now!
f Maybe we can borrow some.
g No way! We can't afford any more.

Dictation

8 **Listen and write in your notebook.**
3.36

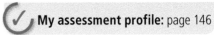
✓ **My assessment profile:** page 146

History File

Oliver Cromwell

These days Britain is one of the few countries in the world with a king or queen. 360 years ago, however, there wasn't a royal ruler in Britain. Instead, there was Oliver Cromwell.

Cromwell was an ordinary farmer until he decided to become a politician at the age of 40. The king at that time was Charles I. Cromwell and the other politicians in Parliament kept complaining that his taxes were unfair, but Charles refused to listen. In 1642 a civil war started between Parliament and the king. Cromwell became the leader of the Parliamentarian soldiers. After many years, Parliament won the war and put Charles I in prison. In 1649 the king was executed.

Oliver Cromwell was now the most powerful person in England, and in 1653 he started ruling the country without help from Parliament. He was a Puritan, a type of Christian who believed that people should work very hard, and that having fun was a sin. Under Cromwell, England had some very strict rules. No one could wear makeup, jewelry or colorful dresses. Theaters were closed, and most sports were illegal. In the time of Charles I, people used to celebrate holy days with special food and dancing. Under Cromwell, they celebrated these days by eating no food all day. On Christmas Day, soldiers walked around towns and cities. If they found any special Christmas food or decorations, they took them away. Most people hated living in Cromwell's England.

After Cromwell died in 1658, Charles I's son, Charles II, was invited to rule England. When the new king arrived from Holland, there were huge celebrations around the country. His journey through London to his palace took seven hours because there were so many happy people in the streets. Charles II soon canceled Cromwell's strict rules. The people of England were relieved that Cromwell was gone.

Reading

1 Read the text quickly. Complete the fact file.

2 Read the text again. Answer the questions.

3.37
1 Why was Charles I an unpopular king?
   Because he made people pay unfair taxes.
2 What religious beliefs did Cromwell have?
3 What rules did Cromwell have about a woman's appearance?
4 How were holy days different under Charles I and Cromwell?
5 How did people feel when Charles II became king?

3 Listen to the people. Who are they talking about?
3.38 Copy and complete the table.

a Charles I   b Cromwell   c Charles II

1	c	4	....
2	....	5	....
3	....	6	....

FACT FILE

Name:	¹ *Oliver Cromwell*
Country:	² ....
Early career:	He was a ³ .... and then a ⁴ .... .
Ruled:	from ⁵ .... to ⁶ ....
During his rule:	strict ⁷ .... about clothes, food and entertainment

My History File

4 Find out about another important ruler. Make a fact file like the one in Exercise 1.

5 Prepare a presentation for the class about this ruler, including pictures if possible. Then give your presentation.

Grammar • First and Second conditional

1 Match the beginnings of the sentences (1–7) to the endings (a–g).

1 If you eat too much chocolate,
2 If you won the lottery,
3 If you don't hurry up,
4 If you lost your mom's phone,
5 If you pass this exam,
6 If you saw a ghost,
7 If you were late for school,

a she'd be so angry.
b your teacher wouldn't be happy.
c you'll feel sick.
d would you give me some money?
e you'll miss the bus.
f you'll be glad.
g would you be scared?

2 Complete the sentences. Use the correct form of the verbs.

1 Would you buy that bike if you *had* (have) enough money?
2 If you .... (leave) now, you'll get there tonight.
3 I .... (not/be) angry if you tell me the truth.
4 If we moved to France, we .... (learn) French.
5 I .... (not/do) that if I were you.
6 She'll get wet if she .... (not/have) an umbrella.

• Subject/Object questions

3 Are these subject questions (S) or object questions (O)?

1 What do you do all day? *O*
2 What happens on Christmas Day?
3 Who sent me this text?
4 Who did she send this text to?

4 Make a subject and an object question for each sentence.

1 Joe gave the book to Penny. (Who/What)
   Who gave the book to Penny?
   What did Joe give to Penny?
2 Penny read the book. (Who/What)
3 Henry usually goes to the movies on Sunday. (Who/When)
4 My friends live near the school. (Who/Where)
5 The small brown dog jumped through the window. (Which dog/Where)

• Past perfect

5 Put these sentences into the Past perfect.

1 I saw him before.
   I had seen him before.
2 We watched the movie several months ago.
3 She drove there yesterday.
4 My friends returned from Seattle last Tuesday.
5 She went to the station before breakfast.
6 He wrote to me last summer.

6 Complete the text with the Past perfect or Past simple form of the verbs.

By the time I ¹ *got* (get) to my apartment, Rose ² .... (already/disappear). I ³ .... (turn) around and ⁴ .... (run) down the stairs. Before Rose ⁵ .... (go), she ⁶ .... (leave) a note for me on the kitchen table. It was a poem. Rose ⁷ .... (write) it several months earlier. But I ⁸ .... (not/understand) it.

• Third conditional

7 Complete the Third conditional sentences.

1 If you *had warned* (warn) me, I *wouldn't have answered* (not answer) the door.
2 If I .... (read) the book, I .... (understand) the movie better.
3 If she .... (not smile) at him, he .... (feel) so sad.
4 You .... (not miss) the train if you .... (run) faster.
5 She .... (buy) the bag if it .... (be) cheaper.
6 If they .... (forget) the tickets, they .... (not get) into the concert.

8 Make sentences. Use the Third conditional.

1 Sarah didn't buy any food, so she felt hungry.
   If Sarah had bought some food, she wouldn't have felt hungry.
2 Richard practiced the piano, and he passed his exam.
3 Jade forgot her phone, so she didn't get her friend's message.
4 Frances and Anna didn't join the drama club, so they didn't perform in the play.
5 You fell and hurt your knee.
6 My aunt's car broke down, so she was late for work.

• Reported statements

9 **Make these sentences into reported statements. Begin each statement with *He said that …***

1 "She loves coffee, but she hates tea."
He said that she loved coffee, but she hated tea.
2 "They've never been to Japan."
3 "We are studying history this afternoon."
4 "She didn't bike to school."
5 "I am going to meet my friends, and we will probably go to the movies."
6 "You can read the book, but you must give it back to me."

• Reported commands and requests

10 **Complete the reported commands and requests.**

1 "Open the door!" (She told me …)
She told me to open the door.
2 "Don't stand on the chair!" (He told her …)
3 "Could you make me a sandwich?" (She asked him …)
4 "Can you buy me a new phone?" (He asked them …)
5 "Don't read your book!" (They told her …)
6 "Give the letter to your teacher." (She told him …)

• Reported questions

11 **Make reported questions.**

1 me why / She asked / in her yard. / I was
She asked me why I was in her yard.
2 her what / she was doing. / He asked
3 them if / He asked / his dog. / they had found
4 us where / the movie theater was. / She asked
5 watching TV. / I asked / they were / them if

12 **Make these questions into reported questions. Begin each question with *He asked me …***

1 "Have you ever written a poem?"
He asked me if I had ever written a poem.
2 "Is your friend feeling OK?"
3 "When are you going to have lunch?"
4 "Will your team win the game?"
5 "Can you swim faster than Sharon?"

Speaking • Giving warnings

1 **Choose the correct options to complete the conversation.**

A I [1] *wouldn't / won't* go swimming in the ocean today if I [2] *were / be* you.
B Why not? I swim in the ocean every day.
A Well, watch [3] *out / about* for the jellyfish on the beach. [4] *Make / Do* sure you don't step on them.
B OK.
A And [5] *be / take* careful not to swim too close to the speedboats.
B Mom! Stop worrying! I'll be fine.

• Explaining and apologizing

2 **Complete the conversation with these words.**

have to understand	I know	I'm aware
let's forget	sorry that	that's true
the fact		

A What are you doing in my bedroom?
B I want to borrow your pink jacket.
A Well, you should ask before coming into my room.
B [1] *I know* that. But [2] …. is that you were busy, and I'm going out soon.
A I'm sure [3] …. . But it's no excuse.
B So, can I borrow your jacket?
A No, you can't! You [4] …. that my stuff is mine.
B [5] …. of that. I'm [6] …. I upset you.
A OK, [7] …. about it.

• Reaching an agreement

3 **Complete the conversation.**

A Mom's really upset. We forgot her birthday!
B Oh no! [1] W*hy* d*on't* we make a cake for her right now?
A [2] I d_ _ '_ t_ _nk we s_ _ _ld do that. We'll just make a mess in the kitchen.
B [3] M_ _b_ we c_ _ go out now and buy her some chocolates.
A [4] N_ w_ _! She hates chocolate.
B [5] D_ you t_ _nk we c_ _ld order some flowers for her?
A [6] T_ _ _'s a g_ _d i_ _ _. She loves flowers.

Review 3

Vocabulary • Adjective antonyms

1 Complete the antonyms of these adjectives with the missing letters.

1 high   l o w
2 modern   a n _ _ _ nt
3 narrow   w _ _ e
4 ordinary   st _ _ _ _ e
5 weak   p _ _ _ rful / st _ _ _ g
6 deep   s _ _ ll _ _
7 light   h _ _ v _ / d _ _ k
8 permanent   t _ _ por _ _ _

• Space

2 Match these words to the definitions (1–8).

asteroid	astronomer	comet	~~galaxy~~
orbit	planet	spacecraft	star

1 a very large group of stars and planets _galaxy_
2 a large rock that moves around in space
3 a bright object in space
4 the path of an object that moves around another object in space
5 a large round object that moves around a sun or a star
6 a person who studies planets, stars and space
7 a vehicle for traveling through space
8 an object that looks like a star with a tail

• Spy collocations

3 Choose the correct options.

1 _tap_ / _decode_ a phone
2 _tell_ / _make_ a lie
3 _decode_ / _track down_ a person
4 _follow_ / _spy_ on someone
5 _make_ / _wear_ a deal
6 _break into_ / _decode_ a message
7 _tap_ / _wear_ a disguise
8 _follow_ / _break into_ a place
9 _take_ / _tap_ cover
10 _follow_ / _decode_ a person
11 _break into_ / _tell_ the truth
12 _escape_ / _break_ from somewhere

• Adjectives with prefixes _dis-_, _im-_, _in-_ and _un-_

4 Put the letters in the correct order to complete the adjectives.

1 r i a f   un_fair_
2 c c s u u l e s f s   un....
3 y o l a l   dis....
4 n e o h s t   dis....
5 p r a t i o p a p r e   in....
6 r c r c o t e   in....
7 t i a p e n t   im....
8 t i l p e o   im....

• Party collocations

5 Complete the text with these words.

dressy	greeted	heels	hired	hair
jacket	limo	put up	~~throw~~	time

Last weekend we decided to ¹ _throw_ a party for all our friends. We ² .... a lot of decorations and ³ .... a DJ. We asked everyone to wear ⁴ .... clothes—a ⁵ .... and tie for the boys and dresses with high ⁶ .... for the girls. We spent a long time doing our ⁷ .... . Some of our friends even went to the party by ⁸ .... . We stood at the door and ⁹ .... all our guests. It was amazing, and we all had the ¹⁰ .... of our lives!

• Reporting verbs

6 Choose the correct options to complete the text.

Jane ¹ _refused_ / _offered_ to speak to Patrick because he had stolen $5 from her wallet. Patrick ² _admitted_ / _warned_ that he had taken the money, but ³ _agreed_ / _explained_ that he had planned to give it back. He ⁴ _mentioned_ / _promised_ to give the $5 back to Jane by the end of the week. But at the end of the week, Jane ⁵ _complained_ / _invited_ that she still hadn't received the money. She ⁶ _warned_ / _admitted_ Patrick that she would tell his parents. We all ⁷ _promised_ / _agreed_ that Patrick had made a big mistake.

Word list

Unit 7 • Final Frontiers

Adjective antonyms

ancient	/ˈeɪnʃənt/
dark	/dɑrk/
deep	/dip/
heavy	/ˈhevi/
high	/haɪ/
light	/laɪt/
low	/loʊ/
modern	/ˈmɑdən/
narrow	/ˈnæroʊ/
ordinary	/ˈɔrdnˌeri/
permanent	/ˈpɚmənənt/
powerful	/ˈpaʊəfəl/
shallow	/ˈʃæloʊ/
strange	/streɪndʒ/
strong	/strɔŋ/
temporary	/ˈtempəˌreri/
weak	/wik/
wide	/waɪd/

Space

asteroid	/ˈæstəˌrɔɪd/
astronaut	/ˈæstrəˌnɔt/
astronomer	/əˈstrɑnəmɚ/
comet	/ˈkɑmɪt/
galaxy	/ˈgæləksi/
moon	/mun/
orbit	/ˈɔrbɪt/
planet	/ˈplænət/
solar system	/ˈsoʊlɚ ˌsɪstəm/
spacecraft	/ˈspeɪskræft/
star	/stɑr/
telescope	/ˈteləskoʊp/

Unit 8 • Spies

Spy collocations

break into somewhere	/breɪk ˈɪntə ˈsʌmwer/
decode a message	/dɪˌkoʊd ə ˈmesɪdʒ/
escape from somewhere	/ɪˈskeɪp frəm ˈsʌmwer/
follow someone	/ˈfɑloʊ ˌsʌmwʌn/
make a deal	/ˌmeɪk ə ˈdil/
spy on someone	/ˈspaɪ ɔn ˌsʌmwʌn/
take cover	/teɪk ˈkʌvɚ/
tap a phone	/ˌtæp ə ˈfoʊn/
tell a lie	/ˌtel ə ˈlaɪ/

tell the truth	/ˌtel ðə ˈtruθ/
track down a person	/ˌtræk ˈdaʊn ə ˈpɚsən/
wear a disguise	/ˌwer ə dɪsˈgaɪz/

Adjectives with prefixes *dis-*, *im-*, *in-* and *un-*

dishonest	/dɪsˈɑnɪst/
disloyal	/dɪsˈlɔɪəl/
dissatisfied	/dɪˈsætəsˌfaɪd/
impatient	/ɪmˈpeɪʃənt/
impolite	/ˌɪmpəˈlaɪt/
impossible	/ɪmˈpɑsəbəl/
inappropriate	/ˌɪnəˈproʊpri-ət/
incorrect	/ˌɪnkəˈrekt/
intolerant	/ɪnˈtɑlərənt/
unfair	/ˌʌnˈfer/
unimportant	/ˌʌnɪmˈpɔrtnt/
unsuccessful	/ˌʌnsəkˈsesfəl/

Unit 9 • Celebrate!

Party collocations

do your hair	/ˌdu yɚ ˈheər/
go by limo	/ˌgoʊ baɪ ˈlɪmoʊ/
greet your guests	/ˌgrit yɚ ˈgests/
have the time of your life	/ˌhæv ðə ˈtaɪm əv yɚ ˈlaɪf/
hire a DJ	/ˌhaɪɚ ə ˈdi ˈdʒeɪ/
make a speech	/ˌmeɪk ə ˈspitʃ/
put up decorations	/ˌpʊt ʌp ˌdekəˈreɪʃənz/
stay up all night	/ˌsteɪ ʌp ˈɔl ˈnaɪt/
throw a party	/ˌθroʊ ə ˈparti/
wear a jacket and tie	/ˌwer ə ˈdʒækɪt ən ˈtaɪ/
wear casual clothes	/ˌwer ˈkæʒuəl ˈkloʊðz/
wear dressy clothes	/ˌwer ˈdresi ˈkloʊðz/
wear high heels	/ˌwer ˈhaɪ ˈhilz/

Reporting verbs

admit	/ədˈmɪt/
agree	/əˈgri/
complain	/kəmˈpleɪn/
explain	/ɪkˈspleɪn/
invite	/ɪnˈvaɪt/
mention	/ˈmenʃən/
offer	/ˈɔfɚ/
promise	/ˈprɑmɪs/
refuse	/rɪˈfyuz/
warn	/wɔrn/

Brain Trainers

Unit 5

1 Choose three objects from the grid in a straight or diagonal line. Write a story in your notebook about what happened yesterday.

2 Read the words aloud three times. Try to remember them in order. Then cover the list and write the words in your notebook. How many can you remember?

front desk	phone	inquiry
appointment	meeting	presentation

spreadsheet	office supplies	making copies
email	report	payment

3 Make eight job qualities from the letters below. You have two minutes.

tie	nt	pa	
re	le	ab	li
tu	pu	al	nc
te	ac	cu	ra
al	ic	an	al	yt
ga	ed	niz	or
en	pe	ex	ced	ri
pr	al	tic	ac

patient

Unit 6

1a Look at the puzzle. Can you find one picture that doesn't appear twice? Look, but don't mark the puzzle. You have one minute.

1b Look at the puzzle again. Find two things to eat and two means of transportation you can find at the coast.

2 How many coast words can you make in one minute? Write them in your notebook. Use the cues to help you.

c_____   s_____ s___

p___   a_____

h___ d__ s___   h_____

s_____   b____ u_____

s__w___   i__ c____ s____

cliffs

Brain Trainers

3a Read the words in the box aloud three times. Cover the box and read the list below. Which word is missing?

research → replace → remove
recover → restore → release

restore   remove   recover   research   release

3b Now try again.

disappear → discover → discontinue
→ dislike → disagree

discontinue   disagree   disappear   discover

Unit 7

1 Look at the pieces of paper. Find two adjectives with opposite meanings. You have two minutes.

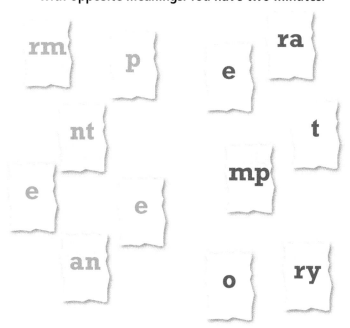

rm   p   ra
e
nt   t
e   mp
e
an   o   ry

2a Work in pairs. Choose an adjective from the list. Act it out. Your partner guesses the adjective and then says its opposite.

high
light
strong
wide
deep
dark   heavy
powerful   shallow
weak
low   narrow

2b Find two more pairs of adjective opposites in the reverse spiral puzzle.

3 Look at the objects in the grid for one minute. Cover the grid and write the words in your notebook. How many can you remember?

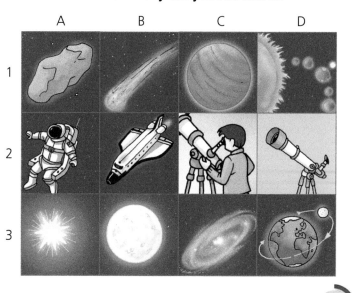

Brain Trainers

Unit 8

1 You are a detective. Choose three objects from the grid in a straight or diagonal line. Write a story in your notebook about a crime you have solved.

2 Make eight spy phrases using all the words in the grid. Then make your own puzzle. Swap it with your partner and complete his/her puzzle.

letl	nowd	onseome	ecdode	a
pys	a	amek	no	letl
ractk	digsisue	owemhsere	ile	reaw
a	epasce	a	sgaemes	lead
morf	a	rutht	noprse	het

tell a lie

3 Work in pairs. Choose one of the boxes below. Read the words aloud three times. Cover them and write the opposites in your notebook, using *dis-*, *im-*, *in-* or *un-*. Who has the most words?

incorrect

correct	fair	honest
polite	tolerant	satisfied

appropriate	important	loyal
patient	possible	successful

Unit 9

1a Look at the boy and girl. Can you find them in the party? You have one minute.

1b Now describe what the boy and girl are wearing.

2 Work in small groups. You are planning a party. Choose a word and make a sentence about how you are going to celebrate. The next person chooses a new word and makes a new sentence. How many sentences can you make in two minutes?

Let's throw a party on Saturday night.

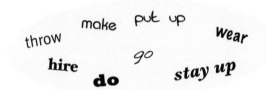

3 How many reporting verbs can you make using these letters? You can use the letters more than once. You have three minutes.

explained

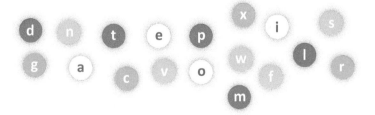

Listening Bank

Unit 4

1 Listen again. Choose the correct options.

2.10

1 Mike thinks the participants in survival shows do *crazy* / *smart* things.
2 Some participants *eat things* / *interview people* that might give them a disease.
3 It *is* / *isn't* safe to swim across ice-cold rivers.
4 Mike talks about a man who *died* / *was rescued* last year.
5 It was *winter* / *summer* when this man was in the mountains.
6 Mike thinks that this person was *brave* / *stupid*.
7 In emergency situations, you *should* / *shouldn't* sleep in a snow cave.

2 Listen again. Answer the questions.

2.10

1 When is it OK to do the dangerous things seen on survival shows? *in an emergency*
2 What did the man in the mountains want to do?
3 What gave him this idea?
4 Why was he lucky?

Unit 5

1 Listen again. Choose the correct options.

2.23

1 Tom's training session starts in *10* / *30* minutes.
2 Tom is scared of *heights* / *flights*.
3 Tom is *usually* / *never* late.
4 Tom is picking up his costume *this afternoon* / *tomorrow*.
5 Anna is going to bring her *pirate costume* / *camera* when she visits the theme park.

2 Listen again. Are these statements true (T) or false (F)?

2.23

1 Tom and Anna have arranged to meet at the theme park. *F*
2 Tom doesn't like theme parks.
3 Tom starts his job today.
4 Anna is surprised that Tom has a job at the theme park.
5 Anna doesn't think that Tom is good at working with other people.
6 Tom is going to wear unusual clothes for his job.
7 Anna takes a photo of Tom.

Unit 6

1 Listen again. Put these events in the correct order.

2.36

a It was used as a school for sailors.
b The *Cutty Sark* was built.   *1*
c It was damaged in a fire.
d It came in second in a famous race.
e It was moved to Greenwich.

2 Listen again. Complete the fact sheet.

2.36

CUTTY SARK FACT FILE

1 *Cutty Sark* was built in 1869 in *Scotland*.
2 It transported tea from .... to England.
3 In .... it was bought by Captain Dowman.
4 In .... it was moved to Greenwich and became a .... .
5 In 2007 it was badly damaged in a .... .
6 The repairs took five years to complete and cost over .... .
7 The ship is now raised .... meters above the ground.

Listening Bank

Unit 7

1 **Listen again and match the speakers (A–C) to the ideas (1–7). There is one idea you don't need.**
3.9

1 There'll be farms on the colony. *A*
2 There'll be one home at first and another one many years later.
3 The colony will be completely dark.
4 People will eat plants from the ocean.
5 It will be possible to play soccer and go shopping.
6 There will be more than 1,000 colonists.
7 The colony won't be in deep water.

2 **Listen again. Complete the sentences.**
3.9

1 According to speaker A, the boats for the floating cities will be much *bigger* than ordinary boats.
2 Speaker B thinks that there will be colonies on the ocean floor in .... years.
3 Speaker C talks about going to a planet outside our .... .
4 The planet would have .... and air that we could breathe.
5 The journey to this planet might take .... years.

Unit 8

1 **Listen again. Complete the sentences with *David*, *Eleanor*, *Eric* or *Anna*.**
3.22

1 *Eric*'s phone was stolen.
2 .... already has some experience of CCTV cameras.
3 .... thinks that cameras are a good idea.
4 .... is angry because the school didn't tell the students about the cameras.
5 .... thinks that cameras are unimportant.
6 .... thinks that classes might be more boring with CCTV cameras.

2 **Listen again. Choose the correct options.**
3.22

1 David felt *uncomfortable* / *dissatisfied* about the cameras at first.
2 Eleanor found out about the cameras *yesterday* / *this morning*.
3 Eleanor thinks that the situation is *inappropriate* / *unfair*.
4 Eric thinks that if there had been cameras in the *hallways* / *classrooms*, they would have found the thief.
5 Anna's teachers are usually *relaxed* / *angry*.

Unit 9

1 **Listen again. Are these statements true (T) or false (F)?**
3.34

1 People of all ages have a public holiday in Japan today. *T*
2 There's a celebration for everyone who has his/her birthday on this day.
3 Azumi often wears these clothes.
4 She asked her grandmother for advice about the clothes.
5 Azumi's parents made a speech at the ceremony.
6 Azumi and her friends are going to a party.

2 **Listen again. Complete the sentences.**
3.34

1 The day is called "*Coming-of-Age* Day."
2 Azumi's *furisode* is long, warm and .... .
3 She has .... the dress for the day.
4 The ceremony was at the city government .... .
5 At the party, they're going to .... .

Pronunciation

Unit 1 • Compound noun word stress

a Listen and repeat. Then mark the stressed syllables.
1.4

babysitter   firefighter   homework   speedboat

b Listen, check your answers and repeat.
1.4

Unit 2 • Sentence stress

a Listen and repeat.
1.18
1 Don't forget to keep in touch when you move.
2 I made a bad decision when I sold my bike.
3 Please try to keep control of your dog!

b Listen again and find the stressed words.
1.18

Unit 3 • Showing feelings

a Listen and decide how each speaker is feeling.
1.29 Write *a* for speaker one or *b* for speaker two.

1 What's that?   angry *b*   afraid *a*
2 It's great news!   excited ....   bored ....
3 Look! A shark!   afraid ....   excited ....

b Listen again and repeat.
1.29

Unit 4 • Consonant clusters

a Listen and repeat.
2.3 spread   erupt   destroy

b Listen and repeat.
2.4 1 The volcano erupted on Wednesday.
2 Don't scream so loudly! It's just a squirrel.
3 Stop spreading crazy stories.

Unit 5 • /ɚ/ and /ɔr/

a Listen and repeat.
2.15 /ɚ/ work   /ɔr/ report

b Match these words to the correct sound
2.16 (/ɚ/ or /ɔr/). Then listen and check.

bird   door   heard   order   serve   sport

Unit 6 • Weak vs strong form of *was*

a Listen to the conversation. Underline the weak
2.30 pronunciation of *was* /wəz/.

A Was there a beach festival here last year?
B Yes, there **was**. And a movie **was** made about it.
C It **was** directed by Felipe Trent.
B Was it really?
C Yes, it **was**. And it **was** shown on TV last night.

b Listen again and repeat. Practice the conversation
2.30 in groups of three.

Unit 7 • Elided syllables

a Listen and repeat. How many syllables can you
3.2 hear in each word? Which letters aren't spoken?

Wednesday   camera   comfortable

b Listen and repeat. Find the letters that aren't
3.3 spoken in the underlined words.

1 It's a <u>different</u> <u>temperature</u> today.
2 Do you prefer <u>chocolate</u> or <u>vegetables</u>?
3 They have some <u>interesting</u> <u>local</u> dishes here.

Unit 8 • /ɛr/, /i/ and /eɪ/

a Listen and repeat.
3.15 /ɛr/ wear   /i/ deal   /eɪ/ break

b Match these words to the correct sound (/ɛr/, /i/
3.16 or /eɪ/). Then listen and check.

air   chair   escape   heat   police   take

Unit 9 • /ʃ/, /ʒ/ and /dʒ/

a Listen and repeat.
3.27 /ʃ/ decorations   /ʒ/ casual   /dʒ/ jacket

b Listen and repeat.
3.28 1 She's studying geography in college.
2 I usually do martial arts in my pajamas.
3 The electrician left some trash in the garage.
4 He just watches action movies on television.

Reading

1 Read about Valentine's Day. What different things
3.42 do people give to each other?

2 Read about Valentine's Day again.
Answer the questions.

1 What romantic thing did the priest Valentine do?
2 When did Valentine's Day start to be a celebration of love?
3 If you like getting cards on Valentine's Day, what job should you have?
4 What is White Day?

3 In pairs, answer the questions.

1 Do people in your country celebrate Valentine's Day? What do they do?
2 Are candies or chocolates part of the tradition on Valentine's Day? Are they important on any other holiday?
3 Are any other saints' days celebrated in your country? How?

4 Write a short paragraph about Valentine's Day in your country. Use your answers to Exercise 3 and the Valentine's Day examples to help you.

Valentine's Day

Valentine's Day (or Saint Valentine's Day) is celebrated on February 14, and it's a celebration of love in many parts of the world.

Early in the history of Christianity, three saints named Valentine were killed for their religion. They didn't do anything very romantic, but stories were written about one of these Valentines long after his death. He was a priest in Rome, and in the stories, he helped a lot of young couples to get married in secret. They couldn't marry publicly because the Roman emperor at the time wanted men to be soldiers, not husbands.

Valentine's Day started to be a day for romance in the Middle Ages, and by the nineteenth century, people were sending romantic cards and gifts to the person they loved. The cards were called "valentines," and the tradition of sending them continues in most English-speaking countries today. People don't usually write their name on the card so their identity is a secret.

Some people also give flowers, heart-shaped chocolates and other presents to their boyfriend or girlfriend. In the evening, restaurants are full of romantic couples. In the US, about a billion valentines are given every year. Younger children often give cards to all their family and friends, and the people who receive the most valentines are usually teachers.

Valentine's Day is also an important day in Japan and Korea. Women buy men chocolates on February 14. This is followed by White Day on March 14, when men buy women candy. Half of all the chocolate in Japan is bought for Valentine's Day!

Culture (5) Saint Patrick's Day

Reading ◡

1 Read about St. Patrick's Day. Name nine countries
3.43 that celebrate St. Patrick's Day.

2 Read about St. Patrick's Day again.
Answer the questions.

1 St. Patrick went to Ireland twice. Why did he
go there the first time? And the second?
2 Why is Downpatrick an important place
on St. Patrick's Day?
3 What happens in Chicago on St. Patrick's Day?
4 Where is the world's biggest St. Patrick's
Day parade?

Your Culture

3 In pairs, answer the questions.

1 Which famous people from history does your
country or area celebrate?
2 Are there public holidays for the celebrations?
3 How do people celebrate?

4 Write a short paragraph about St. Patrick's Day
or another day celebrated in your country. Use your
answers to Exercise 3 and the St. Patrick's Day
examples to help you.

St. Patrick's Day

St. Patrick

Born: around AD 400,
in Britain

Life: Some pirates
caught him when
he was sixteen and
sold him as a slave in
Ireland. After six years,
he escaped and went to France
to study religion. Later he
traveled around Ireland for
many years, talking to people
about Christianity.

Symbol: the shamrock

St. Patrick's Day falls on March
17, and it's an important date in
Ireland. It's also celebrated in
other parts of the world where
Irish people have gone to live.

In Ireland
St. Patrick's Day is a public holiday.
People wear green clothes and
shamrocks, and there are parades
and parties. The biggest parades are
in Ireland's capital city, Dublin, and in
Downpatrick in Northern Ireland
because people think St. Patrick
died there. There are also a lot of
important traditional Irish sports
games that day.

In the US
In the past, a lot of Irish people
immigrated to the US, and St. Patrick's
Day is important there for both Irish
and non-Irish people. In Chicago and
other cities, they put green dye in the
river on St. Patrick's Day. There are
parades, too. The parade in New
York is the biggest in the world.
Usually about 150,000 people march
in the parade, and two million people
stand in the streets to watch.

Around the world
St. Patrick's Day is a public holiday in
some parts of Canada and on the
Caribbean island of Montserrat.
There are parades in Britain, Korea
and Japan, and street parties in New
Zealand and Argentina.

Reading

1 Read about May Day. How many different names for May Day are mentioned?
3.44

2 Read about May Day again. Answer the questions.

1 Why are ribbons important on May Day?
2 What do the people of Padstow do on May 1?
3 Why was 1994 an important year in the history of South Africa?
4 What must the Lei Queen be good at?

3 In pairs, answer the questions.

1 Is May 1 a holiday in your country? How is it celebrated?
2 Are there any holidays with special dances in your country? Describe the dances.
3 Think of a town or city in your area that is famous for an unusual holiday. Describe the celebration.

4 Write a short paragraph about May Day in your country. Use your answers to Exercise 3 and the May Day examples to help you.

Maypole Dance

Padstow

Lei Queen

MAY DAY

May Day is May 1—or sometimes the first Monday in May—and has important traditions in many English-speaking countries.

Maypole Dance
A Maypole is a tall pole, and the traditional May Day dance in England and the US is danced around it. Each dancer holds the end of a ribbon. The other end of the ribbon is attached to the top of the Maypole. The dancers make a pretty pattern with the ribbons.

Padstow
Padstow, a small town in southwestern England, is famous for its celebrations on May 1. There are usually crowds of about 30,000 people. Flags and flowers decorate the streets, and two people in strange black costumes dance through the town. All the townspeople wear white clothes and sing and dance behind them.

Labor Day
Around the world, May 1 is a day to celebrate the rights of working people. There are a lot of protests and marches. In South Africa, May 1 was once marked by protests against unfair laws aimed at black people. The laws changed in 1994, and since then the day has been an important public holiday.

Lei Day
In Hawaii, May Day is Lei Day. A "lei" is a traditional necklace of flowers worn in Hawaii, and Lei Day is a celebration of Hawaiian culture. There are contests in hula dancing and lei making, and a Lei Queen is chosen for her skills in these activities.

MOVE IT!

WORKBOOK WITH MP3S

SPLIT EDITION

4B

BESS BRADFIELD

SERIES CONSULTANT: CARA NORRIS-RAMIREZ

Contents

Work for It

Vocabulary • Work collocations

★ **1** Write the missing parts of the work collocations. Then complete the crossword.

Across

2 I **answered the** .... forty times today!
3 I **wrote** a .... about the problem for my employer.
5 I **checked** .... at my computer.
6 I **attended** a long .... in the afternoon

Down

1 I listened to her question and **dealt with** her .... .
4 I **took** a .... of $175 from a customer.

★ **2** Choose the correct options to complete the text.

I usually ¹(*work*) / *attend* at the front desk at the hotel, but today I had to attend a big sales meeting. I went in early this morning, and I ² *worked / prepared* a lot of spreadsheets. I ran out of office supplies, so I ³ *prepared / ordered* some more paper. Then I ⁴ *made / gave* a ton of copies. After I ⁵ *dealt / gave* my presentation, I ⁶ *made / took* an appointment to see the doctor. I had a headache!

★★ **3** Look at the pictures of Dylan's morning. Complete the sentences with work collocations. Then answer the question.

1 At eight o'clock, Dylan *attended a meeting*.
2 At nine o'clock, he ....
3 At ten o'clock, ...
4 At eleven o'clock, ...
5 At twelve o'clock, ...
6 At twelve thirty, ...

Look at picture 7. What happened at one o'clock? Why do you think it happened?

....

Workbook page 128

★★ 4 Stephanie is having a busy day! Complete her to-do list with the correct form of these verbs.

~~check~~	deal	make
order	take	write

To-Do List

① Check emails to see who's coming to the party. URGENT!!!!

② .... an appointment to see the dentist.

③ Buy a ticket for the concert! (Does the concert hall .... payments online?)

④ .... English report for Monday. URGENT!!!

⑤ Call the supermarket about the job. Ms. Wilde .... with inquiries.

⑥ Ask Mom to .... some more office supplies online. This pen's running out.

Reading

★ 1 Read the texts quickly. What kind of texts are they?

a letters   b articles   c advertisements   d reports

★ 2 Read the texts again. Complete the sentences. Write one word in each blank.

Job A

1 Work is available in the month of *August*.

2 You won't have to pay for eating ....

3 You will work for .... hours total on the weekend.

Job B

4 There were .... bands in total last year.

5 You will work for .... hours total on the weekend.

6 It's going to .... in August.

★★ 3 Which job would be best for someone who

1 doesn't want to work every weekend?   *B*

2 likes Spanish food?

3 speaks Spanish?

4 needs accommodation?

5 cares about the way they look?

6 has had a similar job before?

★★ 4 a Write the disadvantages of each job. Use *have to*, an appropriate verb and the idea in parentheses.

1 (early) *Waiters have to get up early.*

2 (outside) ....

3 (for free) ....

4 (a uniform) ....

b Which job would you prefer? Why?

A

Lincoln Hotel

Work in our popular hotel café!

We need friendly, hardworking waiters to work in our hotel café in August.
Language skills will be an advantage for dealing with orders, payments and inquiries, since we're going to have a large number of international visitors this summer.
You'll work from 8:00 till 2:00 on Saturday, and 10:00 till 2:00 on Sunday. We'll provide two shirts with the hotel logo, which we'll expect you to keep clean.
We'll reward hard workers with free breakfasts, in addition to their regular pay.
The café is going to be very busy, since the hotel is fully booked all August. For this reason, we're looking for waiters who have had some previous experience.
Inquire at the front desk for more details.

B

WANTED

FESTIVAL TRASH COLLECTORS

At this year's Teen Noise Festival we're going to have 65 amazing bands— 20 more than last year!

We're looking for English-speaking volunteers to work for six hours, starting at noon, on both Saturday the 11th and Sunday the 12th of August. No qualifications or experience are necessary. You'll collect trash from outside the international food quarter (selling everything from falafel to tapas!). The work is unpaid, but we'll give you free tickets and a place in a shared tent on the campsite. You should bring boots and clothes that you don't mind getting dirty, but we'll provide gloves. Bring a raincoat, too. We've seen the weather forecast for August, and it's going to be wet. Sorry!

To learn more, attend our Volunteer Information Meeting at the town hall at 7 p.m. on Monday, June 9.

TEEN NOISE FESTIVAL

Grammar • Will/Going to

★ **1** a **Match John's comments and questions (1–6) to Lacey's replies (a–f). Then answer the question below.**

John

1 Do I have any meetings next Monday?   *e*
2 Have you finished that report yet?
3 Can you stay until 6:00 p.m. tomorrow, Lacey?
4 Is that your cell phone?
5 What was the weather like when you went out for lunch?
6 We've run out of copy paper!

Lacey

a I'm sorry, no. I think I'll need another hour!
b Don't worry. I'll order some more.
c I'm sorry, I can't. I have a hair appointment.
d It was dark and windy. There's going to be a storm.
e Yes. You're going to meet with Yola at 10:00 a.m.
f Sorry! I'll turn it off.

b **How does John know Lacey?**

a He works for her.
b He's her teacher.
c They're friends.
d She works for him.

★ **2** **Choose the correct options to complete the conversations.**

1 A Look out! You're going to / will drop that mug!
  B Oh no! Too late! There's coffee all over the desk.
2 A It's cold in this office.
  B I 'm going to / 'll close the door.
3 A Do you feel like doing something after work?
  B I can't. I 'm going to / 'll study tonight.
4 A I'm worried about the presentation.
  B I'm sure you 're going to / 'll do really well.
5 A Oh no! We missed the train.
  B We 're going to / 'll be late for work!
6 A Who do you think is going to / will get the job?
  B I really don't know.

★★ **3** **Complete the conversation with the correct form of the verbs.**

A ¹ *Are you going to finish* (you/finish) work soon, Jake? You've been working hard all day!
B I know, but I ²......................... (give) a big presentation tomorrow. I need to prepare some spreadsheets, but they're really difficult! I ³......................... (try) to stop soon, I promise.
A I ⁴.........................(help) you, if you like.
B Really? It probably ⁵......................... (not be) much fun!
A I don't mind. Look at the sky. It ⁶......................... (be) dark soon. You can't work all night!

★★ **4** **Are the verbs in bold correct (✓) or incorrect (✗)? Correct the mistakes.**

1 It's really cold! It **will snow**.   ✗
  's going to snow
2 I**'m going to get** a job this summer.
  ....
3 Look out! We**'ll crash**!
  ....
4 Ten years from now, I think I**'ll be** famous.
  ....
5 A These books are heavy!
  B I**'m going to help** you.
  ....
6 She **will see** the band tonight. She's already bought a ticket.
  ....

★★ **5** **Complete these sentences. Use the correct form of *will* or *going to* and an appropriate verb.**

1 I think I'*ll win* the lottery one day. I feel lucky!
2 Look at those dark clouds! It ....
3 A It's hot in here!
  B I .... a window.
4 Two years from now, Ash .... science in college.
5 You missed the bus! You .... late for school.
6 Marta .... an important meeting this afternoon.

Grammar Reference pages 118–119

Vocabulary • Job qualities

★ (1) **Complete the job qualities. Write the vowels (a, e, i, o, u).**

1 Car mechanics must be pr_a_ct_i_c_a_l.
2 Nurses must be very r_l _ _bl _ .
3 Scientists should be _n_lyt_c_l.
4 Basketball players must be good
   t_ _m pl_y_rs.
5 Teachers should be g_ _d c_mm_n_c_t_rs.
6 Politicians must have good l_ _d_rsh_p
   qu_l_t_ _s.

★ (2) **Put the letters in the correct order to make adjectives.**

> ### Reference: Morgan Godwin
>
> Morgan is an [1] *experienced* (nexreipcde) computer programmer who has worked for us for two years. He has [2] e......................(xetcenll) IT skills. He is incredibly [3] p......................(attine) when it comes to figuring out the answers to long, difficult problems, and his work is almost always [4] a......................(ractcue), with few mistakes. He is very [5] p......................(tuaulnc), and he is never late for work. His work is always very efficient and [6] o......................(ezinagrd), and you can rely on him to plan his time well. We will be sad to say "goodbye"!

★★ (3) **Complete the table. Write the positive job qualities.**

> accurate a good communicator analytical
> a team player ~~patient~~ punctual

Work "dos" and "don'ts"!	
DON'T	**DO**
try to do everything quickly.	be [1] *patient*
be late!	be [2] ....
make a lot of mistakes.	be [3] ....
keep all your ideas to yourself.	be [4] ....
be competitive and refuse to help others.	be [5] ....
accept information without thinking about it.	be [6] ....

Workbook page 128

★★ (4) a **Complete the article.**

> communicator   experienced   leadership
> organized   patient   punctual
> ~~reliable~~   skills

So You Think It's Easy to Be a Celebrity?

Think again! If you want to be famous, you should

✱ be [1] *reliable*. People won't give you work if they can't trust you.

✱ get as much useful experience as you can! [2] ....people are much more likely to succeed.

✱ be [3] .... You need a good planner to use your time in the best way!

✱ be a good [4] .... , so you can do well in interviews.

✱ have good IT [5] .... Social networking and blogging will keep you in touch with your fans.

✱ be [6] .... It's OK for Rihanna to be late, but not for "smaller" stars!

✱ have [7] ....qualities so that people want to work for you.

✱ be [8] .... Becoming famous takes time!

b **What other qualities do you think celebrities need?**

....

Chatroom Phone language

Speaking and Listening

★ **1** **Put the conversation in the correct order.**

a Yes, please. My name is Aimee Fisher, and … ....

b Oh, hello. I'm calling about the advertisement for a pool lifeguard. Can I speak to the manager? ....

c How do you spell that? Oh, hold on. Omar just came in. I'll transfer you to him. Just a moment. ....

d Hello. Garforth Leisure Center. How can I help you? *1*

e You need to speak to Omar, but he isn't here at the moment. Can I take a message? ....

★ **2** **Choose the correct options. Then listen and check.**

15 **A** Hello, Ballymore Books here.

B Good afternoon. I ¹ *like / 'd like* to speak to the manager, please.

A Who's calling?

B My name is Harry Blaine. I'm calling ² *about / for* the job interview I had last week.

A ³ *Keep / Hold* on, please. I'll ⁴ *put / transfer* you to her now.

B Thank you!

A Just a ⁵ *moment / while*. Oh no! … I'm sorry, she's in a meeting. Would you like to call back later, or can I ⁶ *make / take* a message?

★ **3** **Listen to a phone conversation.**
16 **Then answer the questions.**

1 How many managers are there at Electric Records? *two*

2 What job is Ivy interested in? ....

3 On which day of the week would Ivy need to work? ....

4 Where is Faith? ....

5 What is Ivy's full name? ....

6 What is her phone number? ....

★★ **4** **Complete the expressions in the table. Listen again**
16 **and mark (✗) the expression you don't hear.**

Saying why you're calling	
I'd ¹ *like* to speak to …	☐
I'm ²c....................... about …	☐
Asking someone to wait	
³J....................... a moment.	☐
⁴H....................... on, please.	☐
Transferring a call	
I'll ⁵t....................... you (to him/her) now.	☐
I'll ⁶p....................... him/her on.	☐
Offering to give someone a message	
Can I ⁷t....................... a message?	☐

★★ **5** **Write a phone conversation like the ones in Exercises 1–3. Use these ideas and the phone language in Exercise 4.**

• You are calling about a job. (What job?) You want to speak to the manager.

• The manager is not there. (Where is he/she?)

• You leave a message. (What's your name and phone number?)

• The manager returns. The person you are speaking to transfers your call.

Speaking and Listening page 133

Grammar • Present simple and Present continuous for future

★ (1) **Read the sentences. Write *DP* for definite plans and *SE* for scheduled events.**

1 The office closes at 6:00.   *SE*
2 My mom isn't working tomorrow.   ....
3 The concert starts at 7:45.   ....
4 The stores open at 8:30.   ....
5 Are you studying tonight?   ....
6 I'm going home soon.   ....

★ (2) **Choose the correct options.**

Tomorrow morning I ¹*work / 'm working* at the café. I ²*get / 'm getting* up early because the café ³*opens / is opening* at 8:30, and my bus ⁴*leaves / is leaving* at 7:46! I'm not going to work all day. After lunch, I ⁵*meet / 'm meeting* my friend Kate downtown. We ⁶*see / 're seeing* a movie. It ⁷*starts / 's starting* at 2:00, and it ⁸*ends / 's ending* at 4:50. It's a very long movie, so I hope it's good!

★★ (3) **Complete the text. Use the correct Present simple or Present continuous form of these verbs.**

deal	finish	have	not go	open
relax	start	~~work~~	you/do	

This Saturday is going to be a busy day.
I ¹*'m working* at the museum all day. Work
²........................ at 8:30, and the museum
³........................ to visitors at 9:00. On Saturday,
I ⁴........................ with inquiries at the
information desk. I ⁵........................ a short
lunch break at 12:30, but it ⁶........................
at 1:00! In the evening, I ⁷........................ out.
I ⁸........................ at home with my family.
What ⁹........................ this Saturday?

Grammar Reference pages 118–119

★★ (4) **Read the notes in Aiden's diary. Write sentences using the ideas and the correct form of the Present simple or Present continuous.**

Thursday

Friday

*Friday evening –
video games with Brittany*

Saturday

*the BEACH, all day!!!
8:55 bus
Saturday evening – at cousins'
house*

Sunday

*train – 9:11, home 9:45
soccer practice 2:00
Sunday evening – nothing!*

1 Friday evening / he / play
   *On Friday evening he's playing video games
   with Brittany.*
2 Saturday / he / spend / all day
   ....
   ....
3 Saturday / the bus / leave
   ....
   ....
4 Saturday evening / he / stay
   ....
   ....
5 Sunday / train / arrive / home
   ....
   ....
6 Sunday afternoon / he / play
   ....
   ....
7 Sunday / soccer practice / start
   ....
   ....
8 Sunday evening / he / not do
   ....
   ....

Reading

1 Read the article quickly. Choose the best heading.
  a The Best Jobs in the World?
  b Jobs for Students
  c Three Jobs I've Tried

2 Complete the article. Match the personal qualities (a–f) to the blanks (1–6).
  a friendly
  b a good communicator
  c punctual
  d patient
  e adventurous
  f analytical

Ideal Jobs

| HOME | NEWS | FEATURES | PHOTOS | COMMENTS |

Have you decided what you're going to do after you graduate from high school or college? Read about our three favorite dream jobs, and you might change your mind!

A VIDEO GAME TESTER

What are you doing this weekend? If your answer includes the words "playing video games," then this might be the right job for you. But being good at gaming isn't the only skill you'll need! Being ¹ *f*. is essential, as game designers want you to notice all possible problems to help them figure out solutions. Being ²…. is almost as important. You'll spend weeks, and even months, playing the same game.

B MUSIC CRITIC

Are you going to attend any concerts or festivals this summer? Imagine that you could make money at the same time by writing reviews! Thousands of people want this job, but only a tiny number will be successful. You'll need to work hard and be talented. It's important to be ³…. so that musicians will like you. And you must be ⁴….. If you're late, bands won't wait for you! It's worth the effort, though. You'll have some amazing experiences, and you'll probably hardly ever pay for music again!

C ICE CREAM TASTER

Yes, this is a real job! We asked official "taster" Rob Browning what skills you need. "Well, you have to be ⁵…. because you'll need to write long reports. And I hope you're an ⁶…. person who loves to travel and doesn't mind a few early mornings! Tomorrow, I'm flying to Tokyo—my plane leaves at 5:23! I've tasted popular flavors all over the world. Tomorrow, that means green tea ice cream! I've also tried Mexican chili and—less enjoyably—cheese flavor in the Philippines!"

3 Are the statements true (T), false (F) or don't know (DK)?
  1 This article is for people who've graduated from high school.   *F*
  2 The best video game testers become video game designers.   ….
  3 Testers will have to play a lot of different games every week.   ….
  4 There are thousands of successful music critics.   ….
  5 Music critics often get music for free.   ….
  6 Ice cream tasters get up before 6 a.m. every day.   ….
  7 You can try tea-flavored ice cream in Japan.   ….

Listening

1 Listen to two job interviews. Cameron and Erin want the same job. What is it?
17
  …………………… instructor

2 Listen again. Who has these qualities, skills and experience? Write *C* (Cameron), *E* (Erin) or *B* (both of them).
17
  Who …
  1 is really interested in sports?   *B*
  2 has studied the subject?   ….
  3 has done similar work before?   ….
  4 has worked with people of all ages?   ….
  5 is a patient person?   ….
  6 enjoys hard work?   ….

3 Who do you think is best for the job? Why?

  …………………………………………………
  …………………………………………………
  …………………………………………………
  …………………………………………………

Writing • An email about plans

1 **Read Ben's email quickly. What are the *two* main things he's going to do this summer? Complete the sentences.**

1 He's going to work in a ....
2 He's going to go to ....

New Message ⊗

Hi there,   **Send**

How are you? How's school? Things are going well here, but I'm definitely looking forward to summer vacation!

I have a lot of plans for the summer. For a start, I got a job! My aunt says I can help her in the bookstore, which will be great, because I love books. It will certainly be much more interesting than the office job I had last year. I think I probably spent most of my time making copies.

What else? Oh yes—we're also going to go to Rome on a family vacation. That will definitely be amazing! I don't know what we're going to do yet. Maybe we'll explore the area, or perhaps we'll do a lot of shopping. We're certainly going to visit the churches, the museums and the art galleries. You know Dad's crazy about art! I'll probably send you a postcard. ☺

What are you doing this summer? Write and tell me about your plans!

Ben

PS Some photos of Rome are attached! Can't wait!

Add Attachments: ⊗   **Add Attachments:** ⊗

---

2 **Read the email again and find five adverbs of certainty. Complete the table.**

100% sure	¹ certainly
	² d........................
less sure	³ p........................
don't know	⁴ m........................
	⁵ p........................

3 **Write sentences. Use short forms (*we're, isn't,* etc.) where possible and include the adverbs.**

1 we / will / see / you / there / !   (maybe)
Maybe we'll see you there!
2 we / will / go / to the beach   (I think)
....
3 My brother / work / too hard   (definitely)
....
4 It / be / very / hot   (certainly)
....
5 I / be / going to / do / some studying   (probably)
....
6 you / will / visit / us / !   (perhaps)
....

Brain Trainer

When you write to friends or people you know well, use an informal, conversational style. Use informal expressions (*Hi there! … crazy about art,* etc.) and short forms (*I'm, he'll, won't,* etc.).
Now do Exercise 4.

---

4 **Write a letter to a friend about your plans for the summer. You can use your real plans or you can make them up. Use some of the ideas in the list or your own ideas. Include at least three different future forms in your letter.**

a summer job	a vacation
plans with friends	plans for relaxation
homework	family events (*birthdays,* etc.)
hobbies (*sports events, music events, courses,* etc.)	

....
....
....
....
....
....
....
....
....
....
....
....
....

Coast

Vocabulary • Coastal life

★ **1** Mark (✓) five things connected with the coast.

1 firefighter
2 hot dog stand ✓
3 spaceship
4 avalanche
5 pier
6 cliff
7 spreadsheet
8 harbor
9 ice cream stand

> **Brain Trainer**
>
> We can form compound nouns in different ways: as one word (classroom), as separate words (school bus) or as separate words connected with a hyphen (T-shirt). Use a dictionary to check the correct spelling.
>
> **Now do Exercise 2.**

★ **2** Match (1–7) to (a–g). Then write the compound nouns.

1 sea   a umbrella
2 sea   b gull
3 beach   c cart
4 beach   d shop
5 hot   e dog
6 souvenir   f wall
7 go-   g chair

1 *seawall*
2 ....
3 ....
4 ....
5 ....
6 ....
7 ....

★★ **3** Complete the advertisements. Which place would you rather visit?

beach chairs	beach umbrellas
cliffs	go-cart
harbors	hot dog stands
~~pier~~	souvenir shops

Vacations on the East Coast

Come to Panama City Beach!

The famous ¹ *Pier* Park at Panama City Beach, Florida, was built for fun and excitement! As well as theme park rides, the park offers ² .... tracks where you can race your friends, ³ .... where you can buy presents, and excellent ⁴ .... where you can enjoy fresh, homestyle food.

Visit Newport, Rhode Island!

Walk along the top of the beautiful, wild ⁵ .... , and look down for amazing views of the ocean. Admire the boats sailing into the famous ⁶ .... at Newport and Coasters Island.

Or families may prefer simply to sit on ⁷ .... on the beach and relax! If you don't have your own, visitors can also rent ⁸ .... for some shade on the sand.

Workbook page 129

Reading

★ (1) **Read the reviews quickly. Are the reviewers**

　a professional travel writers?
　b tourists who've been on vacation?

★ (2) **Read the reviews again. Who talks about these things? Write A–D.**

　1 the accommodation: .A. , ... , ...
　2 the people who work there: .... , ...
　3 the bathrooms: .... , ...
　4 the food: .... , ... , ...
　5 the cost: .... , ...
　6 the views: .... , ...

> **Brain Trainer**
>
> Questions may use different words than the text.
> Think about synonyms (words with similar meanings).
> **Now do Exercise 3.**

★★ (3) **a Match the words in bold in the statements to these synonyms.**

budget	close by	loud	~~modern~~
ordinary	pleasant	tasty	welcoming

　1 Joanne stayed in a **new** (= *modern*) hotel.　　T
　2 Joanne thinks that the food was better than **average** (= ....).　....
　3 Danny thinks that the people at the resort were very **friendly** (= ....).　....
　4 Danny thinks that the resort serves the most **delicious** (= ....) food on the island.　....
　5 Keith says that the beach wasn't very **near** (= ....).　....
　6 Keith did not find any part of his vacation **enjoyable** (= ....).　....
　7 Atena thinks that the resort was sometimes too **noisy** (= ....).　....
　8 Atena thinks that it's a **cheap** (= ....) vacation.　....

b Read the statements in Exercise 3a again. Are they true (T) or false (F)?

★★ (4) **Match the ratings (1–4) to the reviews (A–D).**

　1 ●○○○　....　　3 ●●●○　....
　2 ●●○○　....　　4 ●●●●　....

Echo Beach Resort
(on St. Simons Island, Georgia)

Reviews from tourists　　　 Write a review

> **4 reviews sorted by date**

A　**Joanne R, Nevada**　Reviewed 17 July

The showers were broken on the first night that I arrived, but they were repaired the next day. I wanted to stay in one of the lovely old beach cottages, but they were full, so in the end I stayed at a modern hotel. It wasn't too bad, though. I'd describe the meals as fairly ordinary, but the service from waiters and the resort staff was above average. However, the resort prices were too high.

B　**Danny O, Oregon**　Reviewed 29 July

We stayed for seven days. The only regret I have is that I couldn't take a longer break from work! It would be impossible to find more welcoming staff anywhere. The showers and toilets were cleaned regularly. The restaurant hamburgers and hot dogs were almost as tasty as those served at the famous St. Simons hot dog stands—and that's a big recommendation!

C　**Keith McD, Maine**　Reviewed 4 August

I was promised a camping place where I could see the cliffs, but instead my tent faced the street. On the website, the beach is described as "close by." This isn't true. I did a lot of walking! There were no snack bars or ice cream stands at the resort. I spent most of my time on St. Simons Island, which had some delightful cafés and souvenir shops. That's my only pleasant memory!

D　**Atena J, Michigan**　Reviewed 23 August

We stayed in the pretty campsite area. Unfortunately, we didn't sleep well, though, because the seagulls were very loud! Next time, I'll book one of the beach cottages where guests can see the ocean from their windows. Apparently, more cottages will be built next year, which is good news. It isn't a budget resort, but you do get good value for your money. Apart from the gulls, I'd describe it as *almost* perfect!

Grammar • Passive statements

★ **1** **Choose the correct options (active or passive) to complete the sentences.**

1 Most of the world's biggest cities *established* / *were established* within 100 km of the ocean.

2 The coastline of Canada *measures* / *is measured* more than 200,000 km in length.

3 By 2500, thousands more homes *will build* / *will be built* near the coast.

4 Rising sea levels *will make* / *will be made* floods a big problem in the future.

5 Many coasts *pollute* / *are polluted* with trash.

6 Last year around one million seabirds *killed* / *were killed* by plastic trash.

★ **2 a** **Complete the sentences with the correct passive form of the verbs.**

True or false?

1 Caviar *is made* (make) from fish eggs.

2 The first steamboat .... (invented) in the 1700s.

3 The island of Atlantis .... (will visit) by 1,000,000 tourists next year.

4 Over 70% of the earth .... (cover) in water.

5 The *Titanic* .... (discovered) at the bottom of the ocean in 1960.

6 Thousands of people .... (will kill) by sea scorpions next year.

b **Which sentences do you think are true? Check your answers below.**

Brain Trainer

Use *by* + agent if it is important to say who or what does the action. (The city was built *by the Romans*.) Don't use *by* if the agent is unimportant. (The wall was painted red ~~by someone~~.)

Now do Exercise 3.

★★ **3** **Rewrite the sentences in the passive. Include *by* + agent only when it is necessary.**

1 People will build thousands of homes in San Diego in the future.
Thousands of homes *will be built in San Diego in the future.*

2 In 2014, people named Kailua, Hawaii, the best beach destination in the US.
In 2014, Kailua ....

3 People describe Lafayette, Louisiana, as one of the happiest cities in the US!
Lafayette ....

4 They made all *Spider-Man* movies in New York.
All *Spider-Man* movies ....

5 Florida's pretty beaches attract many visitors.
Many visitors ....

6 This summer, over 50 million people will visit Orlando, Florida.
This summer, Orlando ....

★★ **4** **Complete the texts about three coastal festivals, using the correct Present simple, Past simple or *will* future form of the verbs in the active or passive.**

A The amazing Benicàssim Music Festival [1] is held (hold) close to the beaches of Valencia, Spain, every year. It [2] .... (know) for being one of the best pop music festivals in Europe! Over 50,000 people [3] .... (attend) every year. The next festival [4] .... (organize) in July.

B Part of the coast in Queensland, Australia, [5] .... (name) "Surfers' Paradise" in 1933! Next year's surfing festival [6] .... (have) parades, parties, and surfing contests. Many hotels [7] .... (book) months in advance—so don't wait!

C The first oyster festival [8] .... (celebrate) in Arcata Bay, California, US, in 1990. Visitors [9] .... (eat) thousands of oysters last year! Today, all the oysters [10] .... (catch) using environmentally friendly fishing methods.

Grammar Reference pages 120–121

Vocabulary • Verbs with prefixes *dis-* and *re-*

★ **1** Form verbs by adding the prefix *dis-* or *re-*.

1 *dis*appear
2 *re*place
3 ....continue
4 ....like
5 ....lease
6 ....cover OR ....cover
7 ....move
8 ....agree
9 ....search
10 ....store

★ **2** Choose the correct options for the definitions.

1 study in detail: *discover / research / restore*
2 have a different opinion: *dislike / disagree / recover*
3 take something away: *remove / recover / disappear*
4 stop making something: *restore / release / discontinue*
5 find: *restore / discover / recover*

★ **3** Choose the correct options.

1 Help! I've deleted all my files on my laptop and I can't .... them!
   a discontinue   b recover   c remove
2 I .... crowded beaches. I prefer peaceful places!
   a disagree   b remove   c dislike
3 We .... the history of the coast online.
   a researched   b recovered   c restored
4 I was upset when they .... my favorite ice cream flavor.
   a restored   b disappeared   c discontinued
5 I can't .... the ugly stain on this beach chair!
   a remove   b discontinue   c disturb
6 The builders .... the seawall after it was damaged.
   a disappeared   b restored   c released
7 We .... an unusual museum near the harbor.
   a released   b recovered   c discovered
8 We .... the seagull back into the wild.
   a recovered   b replaced   c released

Workbook page 129

★★ **4** Complete the text with the correct form of the verbs. Would you support this charity?

disagree	disappear	discontinue	discover
recover	release	research	restore

SAVE OUR WHALES!

Whales are the biggest and best-loved creatures on the planet, but they're [1] *disappearing* from our oceans. Soon there may be so few that whale populations will never [2] ....

● Sadly, our research teams have [3] .... that some people are still hunting whales. We completely [4] .... with whale hunting. It's wrong! We think it should [5] .... immediately, ending forever.

● Instead, we need to [6] .... whale habitats and food, to figure out how to help them.

● Many seas and oceans are polluted—we must [7] .... them to clean environments for whales to live in.

● Finally, we should [8] .... all whales—those living in aquariums and sea parks—back into the wild.

Please support our charity if you agree.

★★ **5** Complete the sentences. Use verbs that begin with the prefixes *dis-* or *re-*. Which sentences are true for you?

1 I hate it when people touch, disturb or re*move* my things without permission!
2 I love beach vacations, but I dis...................... city vacations.
3 I usually re...................... my school projects online to find out more information.
4 Some people think shopping is boring, but I dis...................... with them.
5 I think the best way to re...................... quickly from a cold is to drink a lot of water.
6 I think we should re...................... zoo animals back into the wild.
7 I don't like my cell phone. I intend to re...................... it with a new one.

Chatroom Asking for and giving directions

Speaking and Listening

★ **1** Choose the correct options.

A Excuse me. Could you ¹*say / tell* me where the beach is?

B ²*Cross / Go* the street near the art gallery. ³*Take / Turn* the first right. You can't ⁴*lose / miss* it!

A Excuse me, could you ⁵*give / get* me directions to the aquarium?

B Certainly. ⁶*Take / Turn* left from here. Go ⁷*over / past* the souvenir shops. Then take the third ⁸*take / turn* on the right. It's on the left!

★ **2** Listen and read. Is the information in bold correct (✓) or incorrect (✗)? Correct the mistakes.

18

A Excuse me. How do I get to ¹**Thomas Road** ✗ *Thomas Avenue?*

B Turn ²**left from here** ...., and then take ³**the third left** .... Cross the street. Then take ⁴**the first turn on the left** .... Go ⁵**past St. Mary's Street** .... Then take ⁶**the next right** .... Thomas Avenue is ⁷**across from the post office** .... You can't miss it!

★★ **3** Listen to the conversation and follow the directions on the map below. Answer the questions.

19

1 Where are the girl and the man now?
....

2 Where does the girl want to go?
....

3 How long will it take her to get there?
....

4 Which *three* streets will she walk down?
.... , ... : and
....

★★ **4** Listen again. Complete the question and the directions. Write one word in each blank.

19

1 Excuse me. C*ould* you give me d...................... to the .... , please?

2 T...................... l...................... from there.

3 C...................... the street next to the ....

4 T...................... the second .... on the ....

5 Go p...................... the ....

6 It's o...................... the left. You can't m...................... it!

★★ **5** Look at the map again. Decide where you are now and where you want to go. Then write a conversation asking for and giving directions.

Speaking and Listening page 134

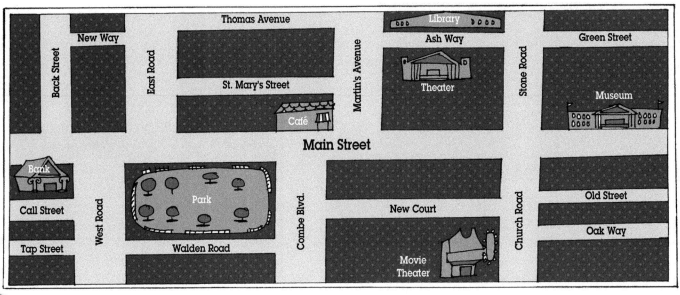

86 Unit 6 • Coast

Grammar • Passive questions

★ 1 Complete the passive questions. Then answer the question below.

1 Traditionally, which pets *are kept* by pirates?
Traditionally, parrots are kept by pirates.

2 What .... the pirate in *Peter Pan* .... ?
He is called Captain Hook.

3 How much sunken treasure .... in the future?
We don't know how much sunken treasure will be discovered in the future.

4 Who .... Captain Jack Sparrow .... by?
He was played by Johnny Depp.

5 In fiction, where .... bad pirate captains often .... ?
They are often left alone on an island!

6 In the past, what kind of food .... usually .... by pirates at sea?
Crackers and dried meat were usually eaten by pirates at sea.

What are all these questions about?
They're ....

★ 2 Put the words in the correct order to make passive questions.

1 When the / island / discovered / was / ?
When was the island discovered?

2 made / ice cream / the / here / Is / ?
.... ?

3 the / sold / When / beach cottages / were / ?
.... ?

4 the / be / shark / caught / Will / ?
.... ?

5 cooked / How / fish / the / is / ?
.... ?

6 will / be / Where / arcade / built / the / ?
.... ?

★★ 3 a Complete the questions using the Present simple, Past simple or *will* future passive forms.

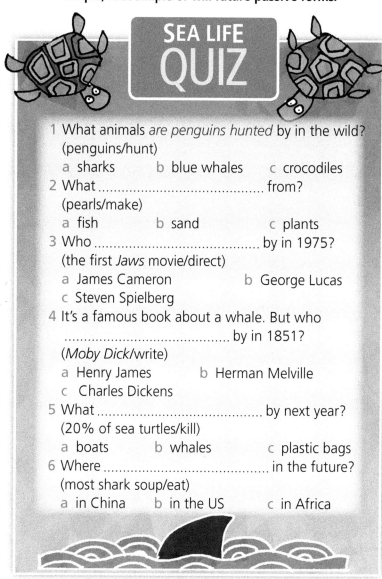

SEA LIFE QUIZ

1 What animals *are penguins hunted* by in the wild? (penguins/hunt)
 a sharks   b blue whales   c crocodiles

2 What .... from? (pearls/make)
 a fish   b sand   c plants

3 Who .... by in 1975? (the first *Jaws* movie/direct)
 a James Cameron   b George Lucas
 c Steven Spielberg

4 It's a famous book about a whale. But who .... by in 1851? (*Moby Dick*/write)
 a Henry James   b Herman Melville
 c Charles Dickens

5 What .... by next year? (20% of sea turtles/kill)
 a boats   b whales   c plastic bags

6 Where .... in the future? (most shark soup/eat)
 a in China   b in the US   c in Africa

b Read the quiz again. Can you guess the correct answers? Check your answers below.

★★ 4 Write passive questions for the information in bold.

1 *When will the seawall be repaired?*
They will repair the seawall **next week**.

2 .... ?
They will release the seagull **on the cliff**.

3 .... ?
People catch the whales **by boat**.

4 .... ?
People visited the harbor **because it was famous**.

Reading

1 **Read the email quickly. Put the places Casey visited in the correct order.**

a a tall building ....
b a theme park .1..
c a beach restaurant ....
d a wild reef ....

New Message ⊗

Hi Michelle, **Send**

How are things? I'm having an amazing time in Queensland, Australia!

On Monday we went to Sea World. Going on the rides was really fun, but the real attraction was seeing the animals. Wow! Besides the dolphins and sharks, there were three polar bears, and stingrays too, which you can feed. I wouldn't recommend touching the stingrays, though. I did—it wasn't pleasant! There's also a seabird hospital, where injured birds are taken care of. When they're well, they'll be released.

On the next day, we climbed Q1, which is a skyscraper near the coast. Builders started work in 2002, and they finished three years later! The views were pretty cool. But the climb was terrifying. We had to go up the *outside* of the building. Never again!

On Wednesday I saw the Great Barrier Reef. The sailboat ride there was OK, but a little slow. However, the reef was so beautiful that I didn't mind. Our guide said you can see it from space! It was sad, though, because parts of the reef are dying. Pollution will probably destroy the reef within fifty years, and we won't be able to restore it.

I went surfing all day yesterday! I read that about one in ten Australians surf, and it's probably my favorite sport, too. Mom went to the souvenir shops instead, but Dad had his first lesson. It was really funny—for me! He fell into the water *a lot*.

Afterward, we ate something called "surf and turf" at this great place near the beach. That's seafood with steak. It's not bad, but you need to be really hungry! We ordered it because we thought it was a typical Australian dish. Were we surprised! It's actually from the US!

I hope you're having a good summer!
See you soon,

Casey x

---

2 **Read the email again. Which of these activities did Casey really like (☺☺), like (☺) or dislike? (☹).**

1 going on rides ☺
2 seeing sea animals
3 holding a sea animal
4 climbing
5 sailing
6 doing an adventurous water sport
7 trying new food

3 **Complete the sentences with information from the text. Use the correct passive form of the verbs where given.**

1 *Three* polar bears *are kept* (keep) at Sea World.
2 Q1........................ (build) in the years 2002 to
....
3 It's possible that the Great Barrier Reef
.... (destroy) in the next
.... years.
4 Surf and turf is an .... dish that
.... (make) with ....
5 The sport of .... (enjoy) by about
.... percent of Australians.

Listening

1 **Listen to a speaker talking about the Giant's Causeway. What is the recording?**
20

a an advertisement
b a conversation
c a presentation

2 **Listen again. Match the dates and numbers (1–8) to the things they refer to (a–h).**
20

1 350,000 *e* 5 200
2 40,000 6 1,300
3 1967 7 1:25
4 1.8 8 1986

a year it became a World Heritage site
b distance from Belfast in hours
c number of rocks
d number of kinds of plants and birds
e number of annual visitors
f number of pirate sailors who died
g year the ship was discovered
h height of rocks in meters

Writing • A field trip report

1 Read the report quickly. In which paragraph (1–4) does the writer

a give an opinion of the town and make a recommendation?

b describe the first place he/she visited in this town?

c briefly explain which town he/she visited and why he/she is writing about it?

d describe another place he/she visited in this town?

A Field Trip to Provincetown, Massachusetts

Last summer my class visited Provincetown, Massachusetts. ª .5. to research why Provincetown is such a popular tourist destination and to consider how it could appeal more to teenage visitors.

ᵇ.... was to the beach, which was very busy. There are several ice cream stands and snack bars. Adventurous visitors can go on kayak tours, explore the local bike trails or pay to go on whale-watching rides out of MacMillan Pier.

ᶜ.... we visited the town center. We discovered many interesting clothing stores, souvenir and candy shops and other attractions, such as the Pilgrim Monument and the Provincetown Museum. You can learn a lot about the Mayflower Pilgrims and American history there. However, the tickets are pretty expensive for students.

ᵈ...., we decided that Provincetown was a popular tourist destination because there is so much to do there. ᵉ.... that the town could appeal more to teenagers by offering more free or cheap activities.

2 Fill in the blanks (a–e) with the phrases (1–5).

1 In the afternoon
2 In conclusion
3 Our first visit
4 We also concluded
5 ~~Our aim was~~

3 Think of a city, town or village that you know well. Imagine that you visited this place on a field trip. You wanted to find out what tourists could see and do there and to consider how the place could appeal more to teenage visitors. Take notes.

1 What is the place and when did you go there?

....

2 Why are you writing your report?

....

3 What are *two* main attractions that you visited? (For example, *the town center, the beach, the theme park, the harbor, the surrounding area.*) Give details.
First attraction:
What was it and when did you visit it?

....

What was interesting/good/bad about it?

....

Second attraction:
What was it and when did you visit it?

....

What was interesting/good/bad about it?

....

4 Can you think of one criticism of this place? (for example, *too expensive, not many activities, no interesting stores*)

....

5 How could this place appeal more to teenage visitors?

....

4 Write your field trip report. Use your notes from Exercise 3 and expressions from Exercises 1 and 2.

....
....
....
....
....

Grammar

1 Choose the correct options.

> **New Message** ⊗
>
> Hello from New Zealand,
> I ⁰ *can't* believe how beautiful the North Island is! You ¹.... definitely come here sometime—I think you'd love it.
> Yesterday we explored the Tongariro National Park, where parts of the *Lord of the Rings* movies ².... a few years ago. Apparently, this area ³.... by thousands of Tolkien fans every year.
> Today we ⁴.... kayaking on Lake Taupo! The trip ⁵.... at 11 a.m., but we ⁶.... arrive at 10 for a mandatory lesson. I hope I ⁷.... wet! I better go now, or I ⁸.... behind. Wish me luck—I ⁹.... need it! ☺
> Danny
>
> **Send**

0 ⓐ can't	b shouldn't	c mustn't
1 a might	b should	c will
2 a made	b are made	c were made
3 a is visited	b visits	c will visit
4 a should go	b 're going	c go
5 a might start	b starts	c is started
6 a mustn't	b could	c have to
7 a can't get	b won't get	c aren't getting
8 a 'll leave	b 'm leaving	c 'll be left
9 a might	b must	c should

/ 9 points

2 Mark the correct sentences (✓) and rewrite the incorrect ones.

0 The cottage will be repaired by local builders. ✓

1 I work at the hotel next summer.

....

2 I can swim when I was only four.

....

3 Watch out! You'll hit that tree!

....

4 When invented ice cream?

....

5 The next train leaves at 12:35.

....

/ 5 points

Vocabulary

3 Choose the correct options.

0 Jess is an excellent team *communicator* / (*player*) / *worker*.

1 We had dessert at the ice cream *stood* / *stand* / *standing*.

2 You should *make* / *do* / *take* an appointment to see the doctor.

3 I came *down* / *over* / *across* a huge spider on the path.

4 Your work isn't *accurate* / *experienced* / *patient*. It's full of mistakes.

5 Let's sit under the beach *stand* / *umbrella* / *deck* for a while.

6 I can't figure *for* / *on* / *out* the answer to this question.

/ 6 points

4 Complete the words in bold. Write *dis-* or *re-*.

A Help! I was ⁰ *re***searching** information for my science project when something went wrong! All my files have ¹.......**appeared**.

B OK, keep calm! I'll see if I can ².......**store** them. There ... I think I've ³.......**covered** the files.

A Thank you, you're amazing! I really ⁴.......**like** computers sometimes ...

B I ⁵.......**agree** with you. I think they make our lives easier!

/ 5 points

5 Complete the descriptions of three vacation photos.

Luxury Hotel in Singapore

Our hotel in Singapore was very beautiful. This is just the ⁰ front ¹ d........................ !

Summer in Italy

This is a photo of a brave ² s........................ standing next to mom's ³ b........................ ! I think it wanted our sandwiches.

Costa Rican Adventure

This is Mount Arenal, a ⁴ v........................ . We saw it ⁵ e........................ with smoke, rocks and fire!

/ 5 points

Speaking

6 Choose the correct options.

A Hello. Langston College.
B Oh, hello. I'm ⁰ *asking /* *calling* */ ringing* about Jed Kane's photography class. I ¹ *would / like / 'd like* to enroll, please.
A I'm afraid it won't be possible to attend a class with Jed.
B Sorry, I don't ² *know / understand / see*. Are you ³ *saying / speaking / telling* that the course is canceled?
A No, but Mel Wyatt now teaches the class instead. The next class is tonight, in the Main Hall.
B Oh, I ⁴ *see / look / watch*! Could I enroll in Mel's class, please? And could you tell me how I ⁵ *direct / get / go* to the Main Hall from Green Street?
A Turn left and go ⁶ *along / pass / past* the library. ⁷ *Go / Take / Turn* the second turn on the right. The college is ⁸ *at / by / on* the left.
B Thanks!
A I'll just ⁹ *pass / give / transfer* you to our Education Officer. She'll take your information. ¹⁰ *Give / Hold / Wait* on please …

/ 10 points

Translation

7 Translate the sentences.

1 The house was buried by the avalanche.

....

2 I'm going to write a report about the harbor.

....

3 We must keep on walking, or we might not survive.

....

4 The old ice cream stand will be restored next year.

....

5 Many animals couldn't swim, so they drowned in the flood.

....

/ 5 points

Dictation

8 Listen and write.

21
1 ....
2 ....
3 ....
4 ....
5 ....

/ 5 points

Vocabulary • Adjective antonyms

★ 1 Choose the correct antonym for the adjectives in bold.

1 **temporary**: (permanent) / powerful / wide
2 **high**: wide / low / shallow
3 **weak**: dark / high / powerful
4 **wide**: ordinary / narrow / strong
5 **modern**: ancient / deep / permanent
6 **light**: narrow / strange / dark
7 **shallow**: deep / wide / heavy
8 **ordinary**: temporary / ancient / strange

★ 2 Complete the sentences. Use the antonym of the adjectives in bold.

ancient	~~high~~	light	narrow
permanent	shallow	strange	strong

1 It's only a **low** hill. We'll climb it easily.
   It's a *high* mountain. We can't climb it in one day.
2 This place seems very **ordinary**. I'm bored!
   This place is pretty ....
   It's fascinating!
3 These bags are **heavy**. Can you carry one?
   These bags are .... I can carry one more.
4 This **modern** tower was built last year.
   This .... tower was built in 789!
5 This river is **deep**. We'll have to swim across.
   This river is .... We can walk across.
6 This sick horse is very **weak**. She can't stand up.
   This horse is very .... She can carry heavy weights.
7 This is their **temporary** home. They're going to move soon.
   This is their .... home. They've lived here their whole lives.
8 A lot of traffic travels down the **wide** streets.
   No traffic can travel down the .... streets.

Workbook page 130

★★ 3 Complete the sentences with these adjectives. There are two adjectives you do not need.

ancient	deep	high	low
~~modern~~	narrow	shallow	wide

Tokyo, Japan, is a very ¹ *modern* city. Most buildings there are less than a hundred years old. Tokyo has many skyscrapers, and they are very ² .... —the highest is 634 meters. Tokyo is on the Sumida River, which flows into the sea in Tokyo Bay. The river is ³ .... , so even large ships can navigate it, and it is crossed by many bridges.

TOKYO

Damascus, Syria, is very ⁴ .... People lived here almost 12,000 years ago! The oldest buildings here have sunk over time, so they're very ⁵ .... Some are below the ground. The Barada River flows through the city. Damascus is in a very dry area, so the river is ⁶ .... , with little water.

DAMASCUS

★★ 4 Rewrite the sentences. Use an antonym of the adjectives in bold. Change the verbs.

1 The building is **ancient**.
   The building *isn't modern*.
2 The lake isn't **deep**.
   The lake ....
3 The water was **low**.
   The water ....
4 He didn't look **strong**.
   He ....
5 It's our temporary **home**.
   It ....
6 They lived on a **narrow** street.
   They ....

Reading

★ 1 Read the newspaper article quickly. Mark (✓) the animals that definitely exist today.

1 Bigfoot ☐
2 Mountain gorilla ☐
3 Mokele-mbembe ☐
4 Tasmanian tiger ☐
5 Hippo ☐
6 Giant squid ☐

★ 2 Read the article again and complete the information sheet.

The Mokele-mbembe	
Appearance:	It looks like a ¹ *dinosaur*. Its color is ² ....
Habitat:	It lives in ³ .... and ⁴ .... in the Congo.
Food:	It eats ⁵ ....

★★ 3 Choose the best options.

1 What evidence is there for Mokele-mbembes?
   a videos   b photos   ⓒ stories
2 What does the writer tell us about scientists?
   a They were surprised when explorers discovered a Mokele-mbembe.
   b Some local people disagree with them about the Mokele-mbembe.
   c None believe that Mokele-mbembes exist.
3 Why do local people think it will be difficult to photograph a Mokele-mbembe?
   a They aren't easy to see.
   b They never leave the water.
   c They are dangerous.
4 What do we learn about the explorers' journey this year?
   a They are taking their own food.
   b The trip may last more than three months.
   c No one has made this journey before.
5 How many different kinds of animals do we definitely know about today?
   a over 5,000   b 1.3 million   c 8.7 million
6 What do we learn about recent animal discoveries?
   a Big animal discoveries never happen.
   b Last year, 19,000 new insects were discovered.
   c Most new animal discoveries are insects.

★★ 4 Based on evidence from this article, how likely do you think it is that the explorers will find a Mokele-mbembe?

impossible / very unlikely / very likely / certain

Explorers Hunt for African Dinosaur

Explorers are going to the Congo to try to find Mokele-mbembes, strange animals that look like dinosaurs.

There are many stories about dinosaurs living in deep rivers and lakes in modern Congo. However, no one has ever filmed a Mokele-mbembe, and there are no clear, convincing photos. If the explorers found new evidence, many scientists would be very surprised. Most think that, like "Bigfoot" in North America, Mokele-mbembes don't exist! However, some local people say that they've seen the animals themselves.

Nevertheless, finding a Mokele-mbembe won't be easy. According to traditional Congo stories, they live mainly in water, and they don't often leave it. They're the same color as their environment—gray. If one noticed the explorers, it wouldn't attack them, because this peaceful animal is thought to eat only plants. But the explorers need to watch out for hippos and crocodiles—these are very real, and very dangerous!

Many explorers have traveled to Congo to find a Mokele-mbembe and failed. Local people believe that the last Mokele-mbembes have died, like Tasmanian tigers and other extinct animals. But this year's explorers feel hopeful. They are going to travel for three months. If they stay any longer, they'll run out of food!

Although their chances of finding a Mokele-mbembe seem small, the explorers may come across other interesting animals. So far we know about 1.3 million kinds of animals worldwide, including more than 5,400 mammals*. However, there might be as many as 8.7 million animals in total. Last year, around 19,000 new kinds of plants and animals were discovered— mostly insects. "Big animal" discoveries are unusual, but not impossible. Until 1902, few people knew about mountain gorillas. The first live giant squid was photographed in 2002! And the Mokele-mbembe? Well, if the explorers find anything, we'll let you know!

*mammal = animal with warm blood and a backbone. For example, monkeys, bears and humans.

Grammar • First and Second conditional

★ 1 a Match the sentence beginnings (1–6) to the endings (a–f) to make conditional sentences.

1 If I discovered a new country,   c
2 If it's sunny tomorrow,
3 If I won the lottery,
4 If there's nothing good on TV tonight,
5 If I were the teacher,
6 If I don't get a job,

a I'd buy my own island.
b I won't have much money.
c I'd name it after myself!
d I wouldn't give my students any homework!
e I won't watch it.
f I'll walk to school.

b Look at the sentences again. Which ones are true for you?

★ 2 Choose the correct options. Are these situations likely (*L*) or unlikely (*U*) to happen?

The future of the planet

1 The world *would be* / *is* a greener place if we stopped driving cars.   *U*
2 If the planet *continues* / *would continue* to get hotter, sea levels will get higher.
3 We wouldn't have as many famines if droughts *don't exist* / *didn't exist*.
4 If scientists explore the ocean, they *'ll discover* / *'d discover* new fish and plants.
5 What *will happen* / *would happen* if we discovered alien life in space?
6 Some animals *won't survive* / *wouldn't survive* if we don't help the environment.

★★ 3 Complete the text with the correct form of the verbs. Use the First or Second conditional.

THURSDAY, MARCH 14

Hi! I'm Max, and I'm an urban explorer. If it ¹ *doesn't rain* (not rain) tomorrow, I'll climb some of the highest buildings in my city!

I ² .... (take) some photos from the top if I see anything interesting. I usually do! If I ³ .... (not climb), I wouldn't see so many strange and amazing sights. Cities are beautiful from above. If you climbed with me, you ⁴ .... (understand).

I ⁵ .... (not explore) a building if I don't think it's safe. I'm always really careful. If I ⁶ .... (fall), I would get really hurt. Luckily, I'm not scared of heights. If I were, this hobby ⁷ .... (not be) much fun!

If you ⁸ .... (search) for "urban exploring" online, you'll find out more. There are some great photos!

★★ 4 Are these events or situations possible or unlikely? Write a First or Second conditional sentence.

1 (become rich and famous / buy a yacht)
   If *I became rich and famous, I'd buy a yacht.*
2 (travel into space / visit different planets)
   If ....
3 (get better at English / practice more)
   I ....
4 (be extremely wealthy / not do any work)
   If ....
5 (have a lot of free time / not have any homework next year)
   I ....
6 (not stay at home all day / it / be sunny this weekend)
   I ....

Grammar Reference pages 122–123

Vocabulary • Space

★ **(1)** **Complete the descriptions of jobs with these words.**

astronaut	~~astronomer~~
solar	spacecraft
stars	telescope

A An ¹ *astronomer* uses a
² .... to look at
³ .... and planets
in the night sky.
B An ⁴ .... travels in
a ⁵ .... to explore
the ⁶ .... system.

★ **(2)** **Complete the crossword with space words.**

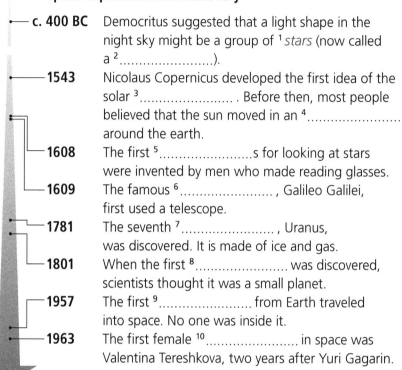

Down
1 something that looks like
  a bright star with a tail
3 a large group of stars
4 a big object that moves
  around the earth, and which
  was visited by Neil Armstrong

Across
2 a planet's journey around
  the sun
5 a kind of very small planet
6 for example: Earth, Mars
  or Venus
7 There are eight planets in
  our solar … .

Workbook page 130

★★ **(3)** **Complete the space timeline with these words. Which fact do you think is the most interesting?**

asteroid	astronaut	astronomer	galaxy	orbit
planet	spacecraft	~~stars~~	system	telescope

Space exploration and discovery

c. 400 BC Democritus suggested that a light shape in the
night sky might be a group of ¹ *stars* (now called
a ² ....).

1543 Nicolaus Copernicus developed the first idea of the
solar ³ .... Before then, most people
believed that the sun moved in an ⁴ ....
around the earth.

1608 The first ⁵ ....s for looking at stars
were invented by men who made reading glasses.

1609 The famous ⁶ .... , Galileo Galilei,
first used a telescope.

1781 The seventh ⁷ .... , Uranus,
was discovered. It is made of ice and gas.

1801 When the first ⁸ .... was discovered,
scientists thought it was a small planet.

1957 The first ⁹ .... from Earth traveled
into space. No one was inside it.

1963 The first female ¹⁰ .... in space was
Valentina Tereshkova, two years after Yuri Gagarin.

★★ **(4)** **Look at the photo. Then complete the text. Write one space word in each blank.**

This photo shows a lot of ¹ *stars*, as well as a bright
² .... with a long tail. The photo also shows Earth's
³ .... , which completes its ⁴ .... around
our planet in around 27.3 days. There are eight
⁵ .... in our ⁶ .... system.
⁷ .... , who study space, have discovered that six
of them (Earth, Mars, Jupiter, Saturn, Uranus and Neptune)
have their own moons.

Chatroom Giving warnings

Speaking and Listening

★ **1** Match the statements (1–6) to the warnings (a–f) to make conversations. Then listen and check.

22

1 I'm going to stay here for another five minutes.   c
2 I'm going to order a pizza.
3 I'm going to deliver this newspaper next door.
4 I'm going to buy her some flowers.
5 I'm going to walk along the river.
6 I'm tired. I'm going to go to bed.

a Make sure you don't get roses. She hates them!
b Watch out for the mosquitoes! They love water.
c OK, but be careful not to miss the bus!
d OK. Good night! Be careful not to wake your little brother up.
e Watch out for their horrible dog! It bit me last time.
f If I were you, I wouldn't order the pepperoni. It's really hot!

Brain Trainer

Write complete sentences to help you to remember how to use everyday expressions.

Do Exercise 2. Then, using your vocabulary notebook copy one example sentence for each "warning" expression.

Speaking and Listening page 135

★★ **2** Complete the conversations with these words and phrases.

| Be careful | Make | ~~Watch~~ | Watch | were | wouldn't |

1 **A** I'm going to eat lunch in the yard.
  B *Watch* out for the insects!
2 **A** I'm going to do my homework in front of the TV.
  B .... not to make mistakes!
3 **A** I'm going to walk on the cliff.
  B .... out for the wet rocks!
4 **A** I'm going to go to the beach.
  B .... sure you don't forget your sunscreen.
5 **A** I'm going to go to the movies.
  B I .... watch the new horror movie
  if I .... you. It's terrible!

★★ **3** Listen to the conversation about Gina's vacation. Put the activities in the correct order. There is one activity you don't need.

23

a mountain biking   ....
b meeting friends   ....
c horseback riding   ....
d kayaking   *1*
e spelunking   ....

★★ **4** Listen again. Complete the five warnings you hear.

23

1 Watch *out for the crocodiles* !
2 W... !
3 Be c.. too fast!
4 Make s.. lost!
5 I wouldn't g..
  if I ....

★★ **5** Do you think that Liam would like to go on Gina's vacation?

Yes / No / We don't know

★★ **6** Imagine that different friends tell you they are going to do activities 1–4. You give them all warnings. Write short conversations, using different warning phrases.

1 go for a walk (warning: alone)
  A *I'm going to go for a walk.*
  B *OK, but I wouldn't go alone if I were you.*
  You might get lost! I'll go with you.
2 swim in the ocean (warning: jellyfish)
3 try skateboarding (warning: fall)
4 have a first driving lesson (warning: crash)

Grammar • Subject/Object questions

Brain Trainer

Try saying questions aloud as well as reading and writing them. It will help you to remember how to form them correctly.
Do Exercise 1. Then say the questions aloud.

★ **1** a Write *S* for a subject question and *O* for an object question.

The A, B, C of countries

A Which country did Captain James Cook sail to? *O.*
   Answer: A*ustralia*

B Where does the biggest rain forest grow? ....
   Answer: B........................

C Which country invented paper, fireworks and sunglasses? ....
   Answer: C........................

D Where do people make LEGO®? ....
   Answer: D........................

E Who built the Pyramids? ....
   Answer: people from E........................

F What country shares borders with Belgium, Switzerland, Italy and Spain? ....
   Answer: F........................

   b Guess the countries.

★ **2** Complete the Past simple questions.

1 *Which famous Italian explorer thought*
  Which famous Italian explorer / think that the earth was flat? Christopher Columbus!

2 ....
  When / Columbus / become a sailor? When he was a teenager.

3 ....
  What / the young Columbus / sell? Maps.

4 ....
  Who / give / Columbus the money for his ships? Queen Isabella and King Ferdinand of Spain.

5 ....
  Who / Columbus / take with him on his fourth voyage to the New World? His son, Ferdinand.

6 ....
  Which Europeans / travel to North America first? Scandinavians.

★★ **3** Write Present simple and Past simple questions. Answer the questions so they are true for you.

1 Who / you / live / with / ?
  Who do you live with?

2 Where / your family / go on vacation / last year / ?
  ....

3 Who / speak / to you first / today / ?
  ....

4 What / usually / happen / on your birthday / ?
  ....

5 Which people / inspire / you / today?
  ....

6 Which places / you / want to explore / in the future / ?
  ....

7 What fact or story / interest / you / the most / in Unit 7 / ?
  ....

★★ **4** Write subject or object questions with *Who* or *What* for the missing information. Then choose the correct options.

1 *Who did a Hawaiian man kill while he was repairing his boats in 1779?*
  A Hawaiian man killed .... while he was repairing his boats in 1779.
  (a) James Cook   b John Cabot
  c Christopher Columbus

2 ....?
  Spanish explorers brought back .... , potatoes and chocolate from Mexico in the 1500s.
  a tomatoes   b carrots   c cucumbers

3 ....?
  .... led the first around-the-world expedition.
  a da Gama   b Columbus   c Magellan

4 ....?
  A NASA spacecraft found .... on Mars.
  a plants   b ice   c oil

5 ....?
  HMS Beagle took .... to South America and Australia.
  a Roald Amundsen   b Francis Drake
  c Charles Darwin

6 .... in 2003?
  .... ate American naturalist Timothy Treadwell in 2003.
  a a crocodile   b a bear   c a lion

Grammar Reference pages 122–123

Reading

1 Read the interview quickly. Choose the best heading.

  a A New Kind of Tourism
  b New Spacecraft Technologies
  c How to Be an Astronaut?

2 Complete the interview. Complete the blanks (1–6) with the questions (a–f).

  a How much do space trips cost?
  b What is space tourism?
  c What will spacecrafts be like in the future?
  d Has anyone tried it before?
  e Is space travel safe?
  f So is space travel only for really wealthy people?

3 According to the interview, what are the two main disadvantages of space travel at the moment? Write two adjectives.

It's very ...., and it might be
....

Listening

1 Listen to an interviewer asking people the same question. Then answer the questions.

  1 Complete the question: "How will life be different in ....?"
  2 How many different people answer the interviewer's question? ....

2 Listen again. Choose the correct options to complete the predictions.

  1 I think we will discover new *planets / animals*.
  2 If we travel to new galaxies, maybe we'll find *aliens / new places to live*.
  3 Pollution will get *worse / better*.
  4 Diseases will be a *bigger / smaller* problem.
  5 The worst problem will be *droughts / floods*.
  6 *Scientists / Politicians* will save the world.

3 a Are most speakers generally positive or negative about the future?

....

  b What's *your* attitude toward the future? Which predictions do you agree with?

Many of us dream of going into space. Now, according to space expert Idris Shah, some of us can make our dreams come true. We asked him for details.

Q ¹ *b.*

A It's just that—traveling into space for pleasure. You'll be able to see amazing views of Earth, or try fun space experiments!

Q ² ....

A Oh yes, this isn't a new idea. The American business person Dennis Tito was the first "space guest" in 2001. He spent eight days in orbit above Earth.

Q ³ ....

A Millions! No one knows exactly how much Tito paid, but some people think it was around $20 million. Unfortunately, if you buy a ticket now, it will be even more expensive! A British company is currently selling places on a space flight for around $340 million.

Q ⁴ ....

A At the moment, yes. If I won the lottery tomorrow, I still wouldn't be able to afford that price! But in a few years from now, things will be different. When people started sailing around the world in the fifteenth to the seventeenth centuries, big sea voyages were new, strange and extremely expensive. Now they're ordinary, and a good value.

Q ⁵ ....

A Well, if you ask me, the next big invention will be "space trains." One team estimates these will be possible in only twenty years. Trains will be able to carry more people, so tickets will be cheaper— about $5,000.

Q ⁶ ....

A Well, there are dangers, but that's true for other leisure activities, like diving or spelunking. Of course, there aren't any emergency rescue services in space! That's why all space travel companies teach passengers how to be astronauts *before* they fly. You need to know what to do if things go wrong.

Writing • An application letter

1 Read the ad and the application letter quickly. Do you think Alyssa is likely or unlikely to get the job? Would you like to do this job?

....

THE SPACE CENTER

Temporary summer vacancies

We're looking for teenage volunteers to join our summer program! With support and training, you will help us to answer questions from our many international visitors and give fun science presentations. An interest in space or science is essential, and knowledge of some foreign languages would be an advantage.

[1] Hi / *Dear* Sir/Madam,

Teenage volunteers

I was very [2] *interested / interesting* to see your ad for temporary summer vacancies on your website. I [3] *am writing / write* to apply for a job as a teenage volunteer at the Space Center.

I have always been interested in the stars, and for many years it has been my dream to study astronomy in college. [4] *If / When* I worked at the Space Center, it would be excellent experience for my future career.

I would be a hardworking and enthusiastic member of the team. Science is my strongest school subject, and I [5] *could / can* speak English, Spanish and French. I am a good communicator, and I have experience teaching chess at school. I have never worked in a museum, but I learn new skills quickly.

I [6] *hope / want* that you will choose me as a volunteer. I look forward to [7] *hear / hearing* from you.

[8] *Yours / Your* truly,

Alyssa Douglas

Alyssa Douglas

2 Choose the correct options to complete Alyssa's letter.

3 Read the ad below and decide which tour you'd prefer to work on. Then write notes in the paragraph plan.

EXPLORE SOUTH AMERICA

Volunteer opportunities for trainee tour guides

We're looking for volunteers to work on our popular tours for young international tourists: the "Nature and History Tour" (Peru), which takes us up high mountains to the ancient city of Machu Picchu; and the "Space Tour" (Chile), where we will explore the Atacama Desert and view stars through the famous ALMA telescope.

Tour guides: You will answer questions and help us to keep guests happy! Knowledge of one or more foreign languages is essential. Please say which tour you would prefer to work on and why.

Paragraph 1: Say why you're writing. (Which tour do you prefer?)

....
....

Paragraph 2: Say why you want the job. (What are your interests?)

....
....

Paragraph 3: Say why you would be a good trainee tour guide. (Do you have any useful skills or experience?)

....
....

Paragraph 4: Say what you would like to happen next. (*I hope … , I look forward …*)

....
....

4 Write your application letter. Use the correct layout and language for a formal letter. Include your ideas from Exercise 3.

....
....
....
....
....

8 Spies

Vocabulary • Spy collocations

★ 1 Complete the spy collocations in sentences 1–6. Each letter of the missing words matches one symbol (●, ♦, ♣, etc.) in the code. Solve the code to discover the secret word.

1 We _f o l l o w_ (✳✚☏☏✚➲) someone when we want to spy on him/her.

2 We tell _ _ _ _ (☏▲□◇) when we want people to believe things that aren't true.

3 The police might tap a _ _ _ _ _ (♣★✚↝□) to secretly listen to a conversation.

4 People wear a _ _ _ _ _ _ _ _ _ (♣▲◇⊗♥▲◇□) when they don't want to be recognized.

5 Honest people tell the _ _ _ _ _ (◗✖♥◗★).

6 We _ _ _ _ _ _ (♣□♦✚♣□) a secret _ _ _ _ _ _ _ (✿□◇◇●⊗□) that is difficult to understand.

Code

◈	●	♤	■	❖	♦	➲	♣	↺	□	♥	✳	◗
z		y	b	x		w		v			f	

⊗	◇	★	✖	▲	➡	✪	❖	✎	✚	☏	↝	✿
					q	j			k	o	l	

What's the secret word? ....
(♦✖▲✿▲↝●☏)

Brain Trainer

Remember: some verbs have two parts.
figure + out; run + away.

Record and review both parts of the phrasal verb.

Do Exercise 2. Which phrasal verbs can you find?

★ 2 Match the sentence beginnings (1–6) to the endings (a–f).

1 The prisoner Mal made   *e*
2 They helped Mal to escape
3 Mal broke
4 Eloise tracked
5 She took
6 She spied on

a Mal down to the house.
b cover in the park and watched him.
c from the prison.
d Mal at the house, and then she arrested him.
e a deal with other prisoners.
f into an empty house to hide.

★★ 3 Complete the text about a famous character with the correct form of appropriate crime words. Who is it?

This fictional detective knew almost immediately if someone was telling [1]l*ies* or telling the [2]t........................ . He didn't [3]t........................ people's phones, because the technology didn't exist in the nineteenth century. However, he [4]d........................ many secret messages very quickly. When he was [5]f........................ people around London in order to [6]s........................ on them, he wore many [7]d........................, including the clothes of an old sailor, a priest and a woman! On TV, however, he is perhaps most famous for his unusual hat.

Famous character: ....

Workbook page 131

Reading

Brain Trainer

Read the title of a text and look at any photos before you read the whole text. Do the title and photos give you any clues about the topic? What do you already know about this topic?

Now do Exercise 1.

★ **1** a **Read the title of the profile and look at the photo. Can you guess the answers to questions 1–5?**

1 What was James Bond's code name?   *007*
2 Who wrote the James Bond stories?   ....
3 What nationality was this writer?   ....
4 Which actor first played Bond?   ....
5 Name a famous Bond enemy with an unusual hat.

....

b **Read the whole profile quickly to check your answers.**

★ **2** **Read the profile again and write the dates.**

1 ....*1908*........   Ian Fleming was born.
2 ....   Ian Fleming moved to Jamaica.
3 ....   James Bond was created.
4 ....   The first Bond movie was made.
5 ....   Ian Fleming died.

★★ **3** **Complete the sentences using information from the text. Write between two and four words in each blank.**

1 As well as writing articles and books, Ian Fleming used to work on *secret military projects.*
2 As well as a military project, "Golden Eye" was the name of a movie and ....
3 James Bond was named after ....
4 .... is one hobby that Fleming and his fictional hero both share.
5 As well as silver sports cars, Bond has also driven ....
6 The most recent movies aren't based on books by Fleming, because Fleming .... novels!

★★ **4** **Mark (✓) two descriptions that best match Bond according to the writer of the profile. Is her general attitude more positive or more critical?**

adventurous ☐   boring ☐   enjoys jokes ☐
sensible ☐   likeable ☐   ordinary ☐
Julia's attitude is more .... than ....

Online *Profiles*

The Name's Bond, James Bond

Profile by Julia Hawkhead

👍 Like

The spy with the code name 007 was "born" in 1952. He was created by Ian Fleming, a writer and journalist who'd worked on a number of secret military projects from 1939 to 1945, including one to track down the German "Enigma" machine, which was used for coding and decoding messages in World War II. Another project, "Golden Eye," later became the name of a Bond movie—and Fleming's house. Like his fictional hero, Fleming also enjoyed jokes.

Ian Fleming was born in England in 1908, but he wrote the "Bond" novels in Jamaica, where he'd lived since 1945. His cold-hearted but handsome hero wasn't named after a war spy, but a local bird expert (Fleming was an avid bird watcher). Fleming said that he wanted an ordinary name, because that's what he thought Bond was like. Maybe this was another joke, because everyone else would disagree!

Bond isn't always easy to like, but he's definitely not boring. It's true that, just like his creator, he enjoys playing golf. But we can forgive that, because he also loves danger, adventure and following villains in fast cars. Although he's most famous for driving a silver Aston Martin, he also takes the wheel of a large bus in *Live and Let Die*! Bond and his enemies may not always make sensible decisions, but they show great imagination in choosing weapons. In *From Russia with Love*, Bond uses an exploding briefcase. In *Goldfinger*, the evil Oddjob kills people with his hat!

Fleming's fascinating spy has appeared in more than fifty years of Bond movies, with Sean Connery first playing the role in 1962. But Fleming had only written twelve Bond novels before he died in 1964. The latest "Bond" adventures are now written by new authors and screenwriters. Is 007 the spy who lives forever?

Grammar • Past perfect

★ **1** Complete the web article. Use the Past perfect.

World's Most Stupid Criminals?

→ In the US state of Oregon, a burglar felt tired after he ¹ *'d entered* (enter) a stranger's home. By the time the homeowner returned, the burglar ² .... (fall) asleep!

→ After he ³ .... (damage) a building, a teenager wrote "Peter Addison was here" on the wall! The police found Peter after they ⁴ .... (search) for his name on their computers.

→ The police arrived after two burglars ⁵ .... (already/leave) a crime scene in Iowa, in the US. But the thieves were easy to find, because they ⁶ .... (not choose) very good disguises. They ⁷ .... (draw) on their faces using black pens!

★ **2** Choose the correct verb forms to complete the newspaper report.

Ellie Good ¹ *just stopped / had just stopped* to speak to a friend in the city when her little dog, Coco, ² *saw / had seen* a cat. Before Ellie realized what was happening, Coco ³ *escaped / had escaped* from her leash and was running toward a busy street! A terrified Ellie called for help—and Spider-Man appeared! Josh Hearn, who ⁴ *dressed / 'd dressed* as Spider-Man for a party, was walking by when he heard Ellie's desperate call. Josh ⁵ *caught / had caught* Coco before she ⁶ *crossed / 'd crossed* the street. Ellie was happy and relieved. "Forget Spider-Man! Josh is my hero!" she said.

Grammar Reference pages 124–125

★★ **3** Complete the text with the correct Past perfect or Past simple form of these verbs.

already/leave	~~be~~	be	close
go	put	just/steal	track

On the morning of August 22, 1911, art gallery staff at the Louvre ¹ *were* shocked to discover that someone ² .... the famous *Mona Lisa* painting! By this time, the thief, Vincenzo Peruggia, ³ .... Paris.

Before the museum ⁴ .... the day before, Vincenzo Peruggia had hidden inside the building. After everyone ⁵ .... home, he cut down the painting. After that, he simply walked out. No one noticed anything unusual about Peruggia, because he ⁶ .... the painting under his shirt!

By the time the police finally ⁷ .... Peruggia down, the painting ⁸ .... missing for two years.

★★ **4** Write one sentence for each situation. Use the Past perfect or the Past simple and the time expressions.

1 She followed the thief home. Then she took cover in his garden.   (after)
After she'd followed the thief home, she took cover in his garden.

2 They tracked us down. It was just before 2 o'clock.   (by 2 o'clock)
....
....

3 Immediately after she found the address, she heard a call for help.   (just)
She ....
when ....

4 He decoded the secret message, and then he burned it.   (before)
He ....
....

5 The criminal escaped. Then the detective arrived.   (already)
By the time ....
....

Vocabulary • Adjectives with prefixes
dis-, im-, in-, un-

★ **1** **Choose the correct negative prefix.**

1 (in-) / un- / dis- correct
2 un- / im- / in- fair
3 im- / dis- / in- satisfied
4 dis- / un- / im- possible
5 in- / dis- / un- important
6 un- / in- / im- appropriate

★ **2** **Phil is the opposite of Sara. Complete the sentences about Phil. Add prefixes to the adjectives in bold.**

1 Sara is **polite** and friendly to everyone. Phil is *impolite* and unfriendly to people he doesn't like.
2 Sara is very **patient**. She doesn't mind waiting. Phil is very .... He hates waiting.
3 Sara is an **honest** person who tells the truth. Phil is a .... person who tells lies!
4 Sara is **successful** at school and work. Phil is .... at school and work.
5 Sara is very **tolerant** of different kinds of people. Phil is very .... He wants everyone to be just like him!
6 Sara is **loyal** to her friends. You can rely on her. Phil is .... to his friends. You can't trust him!

★ **3** **Complete the adjectives. There is one adjective you do not need.**

appropriate	fair	~~honest~~	loyal
patient	possible	successful	

In the 1960s, the CIA tried to train "spy cats." No, I'm not being [1] dis*honest*—this really happened! "Spy training" was so difficult it was almost [2] im........................ ! Cats don't like rules, and they're known for being [3] im........................ . Also, cats can be [4] dis........................, unlike dogs, which are famous for their loyalty! Some people think it's [5] in........................ to use cats as spies, especially because they can't speak for themselves. Sadly, the experiment turned out to be [6] un........................, since the first spy cat was run over by a taxi on its first mission.

Workbook page 131

★★ **4 a** **Complete the sentences. Use a prefix and these adjectives. There are two adjectives you do not need.**

appropriate	correct	fair	important
loyal	~~polite~~	possible	satisfied

1 Please show more respect! It's very *impolite* to listen to other people's conversations.
2 I never get to follow the most interesting suspects, but 008 always does! It's so .... !
3 These disguises are .... for night work. Everyone will notice us in bright yellow!
4 I can't believe you tapped our phones. You're so .... to your friends.
5 It was .... to take cover in his yard because there were no trees or walls.
6 Never read my diary again! Luckily, I only write about .... things there, like music and jokes, so you were probably disappointed.

b **Which of the statements (1–6) were said:**

- by a spy?   ....
- to a spy?   ....

★★ **5** **Agree with these statements. Use an adjective with a negative prefix that has a similar meaning to the underlined words.**

1 **A** Wearing the "right" clothes doesn't matter.
   B I agree. It's completely *unimportant*.
2 **A** I believe he often tells lies.
   B I know. He's very ....
3 **A** She hates waiting, doesn't she?
   B Oh yes. She's very .... !
4 **A** These answers are wrong.
   B I agree. They're all .... !
5 **A** He never achieved anything in life.
   B I know. It's sad, but he was always ....
6 **A** He won't accept any opinions that are different from his own.
   B I agree! He's so ....

Chatroom Explaining and apologizing

Speaking and Listening

★ **1** **Look at the picture and answer the questions. Then listen and check. Were you right?**
25

1 Who do you think the bag belongs to? ....
2 What do you think the boy might be looking for? ....

★ **2** **Listen again and complete the dialogue. Write one word in each blank.**
25

A Hey! What's ¹*going* on? Why are you looking in my bag?
B Oh, hi there! I'm just looking for a ² ....
A Well, you should ask me first. My bag is private.
B I ³ .... that. But the ⁴ .... is that you weren't here, and I really need to finish this exercise before the next class.
A I'm sure that's
⁵ .... You never do your homework on time! But you shouldn't take other people's stuff without asking.
B I know. I'm ⁶ .... that I upset you.
A Oh, let's ⁷ .... about it. Here—you can borrow this one. But please give it back!

★★ **3** **Choose the best options to complete the conversations.**

A The ¹(fact)/ *information* is that you weren't here.
B I'm aware ²*about* / *of* that. But you should never look at people's private stuff!
A I ³*agree* / *know* that. Sorry.

A I'm ⁴*afraid* / *sorry* that I upset you.
B OK, well, let's forget ⁵*about* / *of* it.

A You have to ⁶*think* / *understand* that it was a mistake.
B I'm ⁷*aware* / *sure* that's true.

★★ **4** **Listen to the conversation. Then answer the questions.**
26

1 Where are the speakers?   *at the mall*
2 What is the relationship between them? ....
3 Where did the female speaker think the male speaker was going? ....
4 Where was he *really* going and *why*?
.... because ....
5 Who apologizes? ....
6 Does the conversation end positively or unhappily? ....

★★ **5** **a Listen again and correct the mistakes in the expressions. There may be more than one mistake.**
26

1 You must to understand that I was worried.
You have to understand that I was worried.   E
2 I'm aware about that!
....
3 I'm sure that's truth.
....
4 It is the fact that I wanted to buy you a present.
....
5 I'm sorry for I followed you.
....
6 Let we forgetting about it.
....

b Are these expressions for explaining (*E*), acknowledging (*A*) or apologizing/accepting an apology (*AP*)?

★★ **6** **Imagine that you find your friend looking at your English notebook without asking. Think of a reason for his/her behavior. Write a short conversation. Include phrases for explaining, acknowledging, apologizing and accepting an apology.**

You Abby! Why are you looking at my English notes?
Abby Oh, I didn't understand an exercise we did in class and …

Speaking and Listening page 136

Grammar • Third conditional

★ (1) **Choose the endings that are *not* correct for the sentence beginnings (1–6).**

1 Would you have known …
   (a) if you didn't spy on them?
   b if they'd lied to you?
   c if I hadn't told you?

2 If they hadn't made a deal, …
   a he wouldn't have apologized.
   b she won't help them.
   c I'd have been surprised.

3 The spy wouldn't have seen him …
   a if she'd looked the other way.
   b if he hadn't made a noise.
   c if we helped him to escape.

4 If you'd seen the crime, …
   a will you report it?
   b what would you have done?
   c would you have run away?

5 Where would he have gone …
   a if he'd reached the airport?
   b if the police didn't catch him?
   c if we'd given him the car keys?

6 If you hadn't been so dishonest,
   a she had already forgiven you.
   b we would have stayed friends.
   c this wouldn't have happened.

★ (2) **Complete the Third conditional sentences with the correct form of the verbs.**

ARTICLE

The Graff Robbery

On August 6, 2013, some men went to the luxury Graff Jewelry store in Atlanta. The doorkeeper ¹*wouldn't have let* (not let) them in if they ²............................. (not be) so well-dressed and polite. If the doorkeeper ³............................. (ask) them to leave, they ⁴............................. (not take) jewelry worth almost $40 million! Luckily for the police, while the robbers were escaping, one of them dropped his cell phone. If the police ⁵............................. (not find) the cell phone, they ⁶............................. (not track) down the thieves so quickly. The police ⁷............................. (return) the jewels to the store if the thieves ⁸............................. (tell) them where to look. But the jewels haven't been found … yet!

★★ (3) **Rewrite the sentences using the Third conditional.**

1 Dan went downtown because he wanted to meet friends.
  If *Dan hadn't wanted to meet friends,* he *wouldn't have gone downtown.*

2 Dan didn't take the bus because he didn't have enough money.
  If .... ,
  Dan ....

3 As he was walking down Green Street, he heard Monica shout "help."
  He ....
  if ....

4 Dan ran because he saw a thief taking Monica's bag.
  If .... ,
  Dan ....

★★ (4) **Write sentences with the Third conditional to show how things could have been different. Use all the ideas in the story chain.**

not hear loud noise → stay asleep → not go downstairs → not see burglar → not call police → they not catch burglar → she steal my laptop

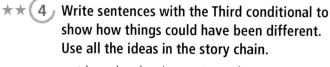

1 *If I hadn't heard a loud noise, I would have stayed asleep.*

2 If I'd stayed asleep, ...

3 ....

4 ....

5 ....

6 ....

Grammar Reference pages 124–125

Reading

1 Read the debate quickly. Who is for the idea in the introduction and who is against it?

   1 For: ....

   2 Against: ....

Student Spies

In several American schools, some students spy on other students and report any serious problems to teachers or the police. In return, they receive rewards, like clothes or money. Is this a good idea? Two students give their views.

Ellie

A few months ago, someone stole my cell phone after I'd left my bag in the classroom. In the end, the girl who had taken it felt so bad that she returned it. She was in a lot of trouble, but the school allowed her to stay because she'd told the truth and apologized. But if she'd been reported by a "spy" first, the school would probably have asked her to leave right away. In a school of spies, no one would trust anyone. Some students might even tell lies about people they don't like, especially if they think they'll get some money! I agree that crime can be a problem. However, instead of training "spies," I think we need more school counseling programs to help students.

Finn

Schools aren't safe. Dozens of serious attacks take place in schools *every day*! Some older students used to bully my younger brother for months. If teachers had known what was happening, they would have stopped it. But my brother was too scared to tell anyone. In the end, he went to the hospital after the older boys had injured him in a fight! The police arrested his attackers, and my brother is OK now, but it was a terrifying time. Teachers can't see everything that's going on. Maybe, if the school had had student spies, the attack on my brother would never have happened. Spies aren't dishonest, untrustworthy people who make deals with teachers just to get rewards. They're people who care about other students and want to help them. I would be proud to be a spy!

2 Read the debate again. Complete the summaries of the two crimes. Write between one and three words in each blank.

Ellie

The crime: A ^{1}*girl* took ^{2}............................... .

What happened next?

After she'd apologized, the criminal
^{3}........................... school.

Finn

The crime: Some ^{4}...............................
attacked and injured ^{5}............................... .

What happened next?

The criminals got into trouble with
^{6}........................... .

3 a Who uses these arguments? Write *F* for Finn, *E* for Ellie and *DK* for don't know.

   1 Some spies will be dishonest.   *E*

   2 Students can discover things
      teachers can't.   ....

   3 Spies will stop most crimes.   ....

   4 Spies can make some situations worse.   ....

   5 Spies protect other students.   ....

   6 Spies will only work for money.   ....

b Decide if the arguments are for or against school spies.

Listening

1 Listen to a radio interview. Who does Martin
27 Fields work for?

   N........................

2 Listen again. According to Martin, are these
27 statements true (T) or false (F)?

   Spies …

   1 need to be good at fighting.   *F*

   2 must be in very good shape.   ....

   3 must be very intelligent.   ....

   4 spend a lot of time following criminals.   ....

   5 need good IT skills.   ....

   6 usually work with others.   ....

   7 have exciting lives.   ....

   8 are very unusual people.   ....

Writing • An opinion essay

1 Read the heading quickly. Then put the parts of the essay (A–E) into the correct order.

"Celebrities have a right to privacy in their free time. It should be illegal for people to take photos without their permission."
What's your opinion?

A ....

Finally, another point to bear in mind is that photographers can frighten people. In 1997 Princess Diana's car crashed while she was trying to escape from photographers. If they hadn't chased her car, maybe she wouldn't have died.

B ....

In the first place, I feel that everyone has a right to privacy. There are times when all of us want to spend time alone, or just with friends or family.

C .1..

Some people think that it should be illegal to take photos of celebrities without their permission. In my opinion, this new law would be an excellent idea.

D ....

In conclusion, my view is that taking photos of celebrities without their permission should be a crime. It isn't necessary, and in some cases it can even be dangerous.

E ....

I also believe that spying on people is wrong. Some photographers take cover in celebrities' yards, or they even break into their homes. I think that this is inappropriate behavior.

2 Does the writer agree or disagree with the statement in the heading? What do you think?

....

3 Complete the phrases in the table.

Giving opinions
I ¹ *think* …
In ² m...................... o ....
Adding ideas and opinions
In the ³ f...................... p......................, …
I'm also convinced that … / I also believe that …
Another point to ⁴ b...................... in
m...................... is …
Finally, …
Concluding
To ⁵ c......................, I believe that …
In ⁶ c......................, my v...................... is that …

4 Read the statement and question. In general, are you *for* or *against* this idea?

"It should be illegal for parents to spy on teenagers' phone or Internet use without their permission." What's your opinion?

5 Choose *three* ideas that support your opinion in Exercise 4. Then write your opinion essay. Use phrases from Exercise 3.

> most teenagers are responsible
> not all teenagers are honest
> parents want to protect children
> some teenagers may behave badly
> teenagers have a right to privacy
> trust is very important

....
....
....
....
....
....
....
....
....
....

9 Celebrate!

Vocabulary • Party collocations

★ **1** Choose the correct option to make collocations.

1 wear *shallow / high /* (casual) clothes
2 wear *casual / high / party* heels
3 *do / make / throw* a party
4 do your *clothes / hair / decorations*
5 have *time / a time / the time* of your life
6 *greet / put / make* guests

★ **2** Complete the party invitations with the correct form of these verbs. Which party would you prefer?

| do | go | make | ~~wear~~ | wear |

New Message   ⊗

Hi all,   [Send]
I'm really looking forward to the prom! Has
everyone decided what dressy clothes they're
going to ¹ *wear*? I know all the boys are going
to ² .... jackets and ties … it's harder
for girls! ;)
Girls—meet at my house at 6:00 if you want to
³ .... your hair and makeup here.
Everyone else—meet here at 7:30, and we'll
⁴ .... to the prom by limo!
We should get there before our friends from the
student council ⁵ .... their speeches.

| throw | wear | hire | put | stay |

BIRTHDAY PARTY INVITATION

Ed and Dan are ⁶ .... a birthday
party at 13 Akeman Street!
We've ⁷ .... a DJ and ⁸ ....
up a lot of decorations. It's going to be great!
We hope you can make it. Let's ⁹ ....
up all night and dance!
Dress code—please ¹⁰ .... casual clothes.
This is a fun, relaxed night, so NO suits!! ☺

★★ **3** Last night Lois went to a party. Look at the pictures and write sentences about what happened. Use party collocations.

Last night …
1 Lois *did her hair.*   (hair)
2 She ....
   (dress/heels)
3 She ....
   (to the prom/limo)
4 She listened to Mr. Brown, who ....
   (speech)
5 She danced and ....
   (time/life)
6 She .... and didn't go
   to bed until 6:30!   (all night)

Workbook page 132

Reading

★ (1) **Read the emails quickly. Answer the questions.**

   1 What happened yesterday? There was *a party.*
   2 Where did it happen? At the ....
   3 Who didn't go? ....
   4 Why? He/She wasn't ....

★ (2) **Read the emails again. What things definitely happened at the party? (✓)**

At the party, guests

1 went for walks ✓	5 danced
2 exchanged presents	6 played a sport
3 wore jackets and ties	7 stayed up all night
4 ate special food	8 watched fireworks

★★ (3) **Who generally liked or enjoyed these things? First, complete the table, then answer the question below.**

	Grace	Ryan
1 the decorations		☺
2 some guests' costumes		
3 the music		
4 the time of the party		
5 the food		
6 the beach game		

What did Grace and Ryan agree about?
They both ....

★★ (4) **Complete the answers to the questions. Then answer the question below.**

   1 Why is the afternoon a good time for a party?
     It's light enough to go for walks and play games.
   2 What did Blake wear?
     He .... and ....
   3 What do we learn about Theo's brother?
     He helped to organize the party by
     ....
     Grace thinks he .... tell the truth!
   4 How did Holly help with the party?
     She ....
   5 Who cooked and what did he/she make?
     (Name *one* thing.)
     .... cooked. He/She ....
     ....

Do you think this sounds like a good party?
Why?/Why not?

....

New Message

Hi Sophie,   **Send**

I said that I'd email you afterward, so here goes!

I arrived around three. The afternoon is the perfect time to throw a party because it was light enough for us to go for walks and play games. I know you'd told me that beach volleyball was fast, but I didn't realize *how* fast! The other players had fun, though—they must be in better shape than me. ;)

Holly had made some decorations (which were not very good!), and Mal, Blake and Chris decided to look like idiots and wear surfer shirts and shorts. But except for that, the "Hawaiian" theme wasn't too embarrassing! I certainly can't complain about the food ... Mmm!

Theo's brother had hired a DJ, who set up speakers and lights on the beach. Theo said that the DJ had worked in Miami, although you can't always believe everything Theo says! Everyone went wild to the music, though—including me. ;)

Get well soon!

Grace xxx

New Message

Hi Sophie,   **Send**

Everyone told me to say "hi"—we all missed you!

Holly had made flower and coconut decorations. She's such a good artist! Most people wore casual, everyday clothes, but Blake and his friends dressed like Hawaiian surfer dudes! Actually, they didn't look bad, but don't tell them that I said so. When it got dark, Jess's dad lit a fire and organized a barbecue. His Hawaiian pineapple kebabs were awesome!

I didn't really get into the music because rock's more my thing, but it was fun getting together with everyone at the beach, especially when we played volleyball! Everything ended too early, though. People want to stay up at a party!

I hope you're feeling better! Give me a call soon, OK?

Ryan

Grammar • Reported statements

★ (1) **Choose the correct options to report what people said about Ed's party. Then answer the question.**

1 Marina said that she *is* /(*was*) having a great time *now* /(*then*).
2 Jose *said* / *told* Zainab that *I* / *he* had been to better parties.
3 Rosie said that she *can't* / *couldn't* stand the other guests *here* / *there*.
4 Oscar told Zainab that he *is* / *was* going to dance all night *this night* / *that night*.
5 The twins *said* / *told* that *we* / *they* hadn't known about Ed's awful taste in music.

Which two guests are enjoying Ed's party the most? ....

★★ (2) **Are the reported speech sentences correct (✓) or incorrect (✗)? Rewrite the incorrect sentences.**

1 Tom: "I'm having a party tomorrow."
Tom said that he is having a party the next day. ✗
Tom said that he was having a party the next day.
2 me: "I won't be home until late today."
I said that I won't be home until late this day. ....
....
3 you → us: "You must put the decorations up next week."
You told us that we had to put the decorations up the following week. ....
....
....
4 we → they: "The DJ won't play here."
We said them that the DJ won't play there. ....
....
5 Ben: "I've known Kate since we were young."
Ben said that he'd known Kate since they were young. ....
....

• Reported commands and requests

★★ (3) **Complete the reported commands and requests. Who do you think might say these things at a party?**

1 "Please turn the music down."
They asked us *to turn* the music down.
2 "Take your shoes off!"
She told me .... my shoes off.
3 "Don't go into the bedrooms!"
They told guests .... into the bedrooms.
4 "Can you clean up, please?"
He asked us ....
5 "Don't move the furniture."
They told me .... the furniture.
6 "Please go home now!"
He asked us .... then.

> **Brain Trainer**
>
> When you rewrite a sentence, make sure that the second sentence has exactly the same meaning as the first sentence. Read both sentences carefully afterward to check.
>
> **Now do Exercise 4.**

★★ (4) **Read the dialogue and decide whether the sentences are commands or requests. Rewrite the sentences in reported speech.**

Mom ¹Hurry up! You're going to be late!
Josh I'm coming! Mom, ²can you give me a ride, please?
Mom Oh, OK, just this once! ³Get in the car.
Josh Thanks! ... And ⁴can you play some different music? I can't stand Coldplay!
Mom No! ⁵Don't change my music. If you don't like it, you can get out and walk.
Josh OK, fine! But ⁶please don't play it too loudly when we arrive. I don't want my friends to hear ...

1 Josh's *mom told him to hurry up.*
2 Josh ....
3 Josh's mom ....
4 Josh ....
5 Josh's mom ....
6 Josh .... when they arrived.

Grammar Reference pages 126–127

Vocabulary • Reporting verbs

Brain Trainer

Learn and use a variety of verbs to sound more interesting. For example, how many different alternatives to *say* and *tell* can you think of?
Now do Exercise 1.

★ (1) **Match the verbs (1–6) to the definitions (a–f).**

1 warn   *c*
2 refuse
3 promise
4 complain
5 explain
6 invite

a ask someone to go to an event
b say that you're annoyed about something
c tell someone about something bad that might happen
d say that you won't do something
e give information to help someone understand something
f say that you'll definitely do something

★ (2) **Which verb *can't* complete each sentence?**

1 I .... him not to be late.
  a told   b warned   ⓒ complained
2 She .... to help him organize a party.
  a offered   b refused   c invited
3 They .... that they were going to the festival.
  a warned   b mentioned   c explained
4 We .... my grandma to stay over for Christmas.
  a invited   b asked   c offered
5 He .... that the party was very noisy.
  a warned   b complained   c admitted
6 My parents .... to pay for a limo!
  a agreed   b invited   c promised

★★ (3) **Complete the second sentence so that it has the same meaning as the first. Then answer the question.**

1 Matt: "You're always breaking things, James!"
  Matt complained *that James was always breaking things.*
2 James: "I'll pay to fix it."
  James promised ....
3 Dora: "I won't lend James any money this time!"
  Dora refused ....
4 Ben: "I don't think it's an expensive table."
  Ben mentioned ....
5 Katy: "James was only dancing."
  Katy explained ....
6 Emma: "Everyone—my parents just arrived!"
  Emma warned ....

What happened?   ....

★★ (4) **Rewrite the underlined phrases in reported speech using these verbs.**

| admitted | complained | explained | ~~invited~~ |
| offered | promised | refused | |

A ¹ Would you like to come to my party this weekend, Brooke?
B Sounds great! ² I'll bring some music, if you like.
A Thanks, but that's OK. ³ My sister's organizing the music.
B OK. ⁴ I'll bring some food! I'll make something special.
A Um … the thing is … I'm sorry, Brooke, but ⁵ I don't really like your cooking.
B Oh. Well, if that's how you feel, then ⁶ I'm not going to your party.
A What? Don't be silly, Brooke. ⁷ You're being really selfish …

1 Aaron *invited Brooke to come to his party that weekend.*
2 Brooke .... , if Aaron wanted her to.
3 Aaron ....
4 Brooke ....
5 Aaron ....
6 Brooke ....
7 Aaron ....

Chatroom Reaching an agreement

Speaking and Listening

★ **(1)** **Choose the best options to complete the dialogue.**
28 **Then listen and check.**

W What do you feel like doing for Mardi Gras tomorrow, Eli?
E I think we ¹*could / should* watch the parades. That's what New Orleans is famous for!
W That's a good ²*idea / thought*. ³*Maybe / Possibly* we can join in the dancing, too!
E ⁴*No / Not* way! You know I hate dancing, Willow. ⁵*How / Why* don't we have lunch afterward, and eat some Cajun food? We'll probably be hungry!
W That ⁶*does / makes* sense. OK, let's do that. Do you think we ⁷*could / may* take a bus there?
E No, I don't ⁸*agree / think* we should do that. Most of the streets will be closed! Let's walk. We can listen to the jazz bands on the way!

★ **(2)** **Complete the conversations with these words.**

a good idea	Maybe we	sense	way
~~we could~~	we should (x2)	Why don't	

1 **A** Do you think *we could* go by limo?
  B No .... ! Limos are too expensive.
2 **A** I think .... all wear casual clothes.
  B That makes .... It's a party, not a prom!
3 **A** .... we walk?
  B I don't think .... walk there in the dark.
4 **A** .... can bring our own food.
  B That's .... It'll be cheaper.

★★ **(3)** **Gabriel and Carla are organizing a surprise birthday party**
29 **for their friend Yasmin. Listen and mark (✓) the problems you hear. Then answer the question.**

1 There isn't a DJ.
2 The guests are too busy to come.
3 There isn't any food.
4 There isn't a cake.
5 There aren't any decorations.
6 Someone hasn't been invited.

What is the biggest problem? Why?

....

★★ **(4)** **a Listen again. Who says**
29 **these sentences, Gabriel (G) or Carla (C)?**

1 Do you think we could play the music ourselves?   *G, S*
2 That makes sense.   ....
3 Maybe we can buy one.
   ....
4 That's a great idea.   ....
5 No way!   ....
6 I don't think we should have black decorations.
   ....
7 Why don't we put up these?   ....
8 I think you should call her.
   ....

b Are the sentences making suggestions (S), agreeing (A) or disagreeing (D)?

★★ **(5)** **It's almost the last day of the school year. Imagine that you and a friend want to do something special on the weekend to celebrate the beginning of summer break. Write the conversation. Use the ideas below and expressions from Exercises 1 and 2.**

Your friend suggests an activity. (What?)
You aren't interested. (Why?)
You suggest an activity. (What?)
Your friend likes your idea.
Now agree when and where to meet.

Speaking and Listening page 137

Grammar • Reported questions

★ **1** a **Choose the correct reported questions.**

1 "What time does the party start?"
   a) She asked me what time the party started.
   b She asked me what time started the party.

2 "Did you have a good time?"
   a I asked him that he'd had a good time.
   b I asked him if he'd had a good time.

3 "Where can we put our coats?"
   a They asked me where could they put their coats.
   b They asked me where they could put their coats.

4 "How are you getting home?"
   a Elsie asked us how we were getting home.
   b Elsie asked us if we were getting home.

5 "Do I have to wear dressy clothes?"
   a You asked her if you had to wear dressy clothes.
   b You asked her if you did have to wear dressy clothes.

6 "Will you need a taxi?"
   a Jamie asked me if I would a taxi need.
   b Jamie asked me if I would need a taxi.

b **Which of the questions were asked by**

party guests?   ..1...................
party organizers?   ....

★ **2** **Rewrite the reported questions in direct speech. Remember to change the words in bold as well as the word order.**

1 Tom asked her if **she was enjoying** the party.
   "*Are you enjoying* the party?" Tom asked her.

2 Mom asked what time everyone **was going** to arrive.
   "What time ....
   to arrive?" Mom asked.

3 They asked us if **they could help**.
   "......................................?" they asked us.

4 Robin asked me what time the limo **would arrive**.
   "......................................?" Robin asked me.

5 Kelly asked me if **I wanted** to dance.
   "...................................... to dance?" Kelly asked me.

Grammar Reference pages 126–127

★★ **3** **Write a reported question for each answer. Look at the words in bold to decide if you need to include a question word or expression.**

1 Belle asked *Aiden if he wanted any more cake.*
   "**No**, I don't want any more cake," said Aiden.

2 Kayla asked ....
   "**Jackson** chose the music," I told her.

3 Blake asked ....
   "**Yes**, we're going to come tonight," we promised.

4 I asked ....
   "The bathroom is **on the left**," Aimee explained.

5 Jack's sisters asked ....
   "**No**, I didn't enjoy the prom last night!" complained Jack.

6 We asked ....
   "I've been a DJ **for five years**," Ella told us.

★★ **4** **Imagine you're a Hollywood celebrity! Rewrite the questions in reported speech. What would you reply?**

1 **"What skills do the best actors have to have?"**
   Planet newspaper

2 **"Have you ever had any other jobs?"**
   Shh! website

3 "Will you star in any exciting new movies soon?"
   Starz website

4 **"Which character are you going to play next?"**
   The Art Show

5 **"How did you become famous?"** *a fan*

6 **"Do you enjoy your fame?"** *Hiya magazine*

7 **"Where are you living?"** *Celeb Living blog*

1 *Planet newspaper asked me what skills the best actors had to have.*

2 ....
3 ....
4 ....
5 ....
6 ....
7 ....

Reading

1 Read the What's On guide quickly. Which events might these festival visitors enjoy the most?

1 Alex loves sports.
2 Veronica is into comedy.
3 Josh wants to see a concert.
4 Fabio likes movies.

2 Read the What's On guide again. Complete the blanks (1–7) with the missing sentences (a–g).

a Back there, she's already becoming a celebrity.
b For this reason, you'll need to bring your ID.
c In this beautiful setting, the music sounds magical.
d In Edinburgh, that means it's time for the biggest cultural festival in the world!
e And they'll do *anything* to win!
f Not in these highly competitive events!
g You'll be amazed by their fire and light displays.

3 According to evidence in the guide, which event or events

1 might encourage people to change their opinion of something?
Roller Derby, ...
2 may feature people who are dressed in unusual clothes?
.... , ...
3 won't be appropriate for people of all ages?
....
4 might have a negative consequence for some visitors?
.... , ...

WHAT'S ON AT THE EDINBURGH FESTIVAL

Galaxy Readers' Recommendations

It's August. ¹ *d.* Last week we asked our readers to send in recommendations for the most "must-see" events …

One Strange Lady

Clarissa Beddoes is performing her very funny and highly unusual show "One Strange Lady" for the first time outside her homeland, the US. ² .... Book tickets now if you want to find out why. There aren't many left! Readers who saw the show on her first night complained that their faces hurt afterward because they'd laughed so much!

Scream Night

Stay up all night and watch all the best horror nonstop! The organizers promise to terrify you … in a good way! Readers have told us that last year's event was a lot of fun, with many fans wearing costumes to the theater. Shows are rated for ages 15+ from 11 a.m. to 9 p.m., and for ages 18+ only after 9 p.m. ³ .... For example, your student card or a passport.

Roller Derby

Skating is a relaxing leisure activity, right? ⁴ .... Roller derbies are *fast* and really fun to watch. The all-women teams wear colorful punk outfits and give themselves names like "Killer Queen." ⁵ .... As a result, crashes happen regularly. Readers have warned us not to sit too close to the front, to avoid accidents!

Fireworks Finale

Many of you said that this was your favorite yearly event! Listen to the Scottish Chamber Orchestra play at the castle on the hill. ⁶ .... Even *more* magic is added by firework artists. ⁷ .... They're absolutely stunning. Don't worry if classical music isn't usually "your thing." Many readers have told us that this event made them think again!

Listening

1 Listen to three friends discussing what to do at the Edinburgh festival. Number these events in the order you hear them. Which event do they decide to go to?

a a concert ....   c a comedy show ....
b a sports event ....   d a movie night *1.*

2 Listen again and complete the table. Which event would *you* prefer?

Event	Cost	Reason for going/not going
1	£6	It sounds *boring*.
2	£.........	The performer isn't very ....
3	£.........	It's too ....
4	£.........	The tickets are .... and the food is ....

Writing • A problem page

1 Read the problem and the reply. Complete the summary sentences.

Problem: Maya had a ¹*party*. Afterward, her parents were ² .... !
Advice: You could offer to help pay for any damage. You could do ³ ....
You should ⁴ ....

Problem Page

Dear Dave,

My birthday party was a disaster! The night before, I'd mentioned the party online. ¹ That was a mistake because a lot of extra guests arrived. Some of ² them made a mess in the house and broke a few things! Mom and Dad were furious. ³ They told me I couldn't have any friends over until they could trust me again. That was a month ago! What should I do?

Maya

Dear Maya,

I'm sorry to hear about your problem. I'm sure you feel bad about what happened, and that you won't make the same mistake in the future! Social networking sites can be fun, but ⁴ they aren't the right places to invite guests to a party—as you found out!

Have you offered to help pay for any damage? You could get a weekend job to earn some money. Why don't you try doing some extra housework at home, too? ⁵ It might show your parents how responsible you are. Finally, ⁶ my main piece of advice is to talk to your parents about the situation. Promise never to throw a party like that again, and ask them what you should do to win back ⁷ their trust.

Good luck. ⁸ Your parents won't stay angry forever!

Dave

---

2 Look at the <u>underlined</u> pronouns and possessive adjectives (1–8) in the problem page. Match them to the meanings (a–h).

Pronouns
a Maya's parents
b mentioning the party online   *1*
c doing extra housework
d social networking sites
e the extra guests

Possessive adjectives
f relating to Maya
g relating to Dave
h relating to Maya's parents

3 Read the problem. Then read the advice below. What are your three favorite suggestions? You can choose your own ideas if you prefer.

Hello,

I really hope you can help! My best friend, Sandra, is going to a music festival next weekend with her brother and sister, who are 19 and 20. A lot of my favorite bands are going to play there, but my parents have refused to let me go! They say I'm not old enough. What should I do? I really want to go!

Jackson, 16

- promise not to stay up all night
- explain how important the festival is to you
- promise to text or call them from the festival
- introduce them to Sandra's brother and sister
- show them the festival website—especially the section about rules and safety!
- agree to do extra housework to prove that you're responsible
- promise to pay for the tickets yourself

4 Write a reply to the problem in Exercise 3. Use the paragraph plan below to help you. Include pronouns and possessive adjectives so that you don't repeat ideas.

Paragraph 1: Express sympathy with the writer.

Paragraph 2: Give advice, explaining your ideas. Include at least *three* pieces of advice.

Paragraph 3: End with some positive words and give some final advice.

Dear Jackson,

....
....
....
....
....
....
....
....
....
....
....

Check 3

Grammar

1 Complete the sentences with the correct form of the verbs.

0 If we wait too long, we *will miss* the bus. (miss)

1 I asked him if he .... help me to write a speech. (can)

2 I .... to go into space if I were rich. (love)

3 By the time the police tracked him down, he .... off his disguise. (already/take)

4 I .... to the party if he doesn't invite me. (not go)

5 If they .... (not tap) his phone, they wouldn't have learned the truth.

6 She asked her guests .... dressy clothes. (wear)

| / 6 points |

2 Write the questions. Use *Who* or *What* and the correct Past simple form of the verb. Add an object (*you*) if necessary.

A 0 *Who took* this photo? (take)

B My mom. It was a special day!

A Why? 1 .... ? (happen)

B I passed all my exams!

A Congratulations!
2 .... next? (do)

B I had a party, of course!

A 3 .... ? (invite)

B I invited my whole class.

A 4 .... ? (come)

B Everyone!

| / 4 points |

3 Rewrite the second sentence so that it has a similar meaning to the first one.

0 "Don't follow me," Tony told her.
Tony told her *not to follow him*.

1 "Why have you been so disloyal to me?" I asked her.
I asked her ....

2 The limo left. Then I arrived.
By the time I arrived, ...

3 "I'll hire a DJ tomorrow," he said.
He said that ....

4 She decoded the message and caught the criminal.
If she hadn't ....

5 "Did you go to the party yesterday?" they asked me.
They asked me ....

| / 5 points |

Vocabulary

4 Choose the correct options.

American Teen Wins "Out of This World" Prize

When Marcie Gray from the Space Agency called 18-year-old Dylan Hollings and told him that he'd won a trip into space, he thought she was 0. C. lies! "At first I was a little 1.... polite to Marcie," he says. "I thought it was a joke!" Eventually, he realized that Marcie was telling the 2.... , and that nothing she'd said had been 3....correct in any way. He really was going to take a seat inside a 4.... and travel in an 5.... around the Earth!

The agency has 6.... Dylan to attend a three-month space training course, and Marcie has 7.... him that space travel isn't for everyone. The power of gravity isn't as 8.... in space (it's much weaker), so it's more difficult to do 9.... , everyday things, like eating and walking. But Dylan is excited. "I'm going to 10.... the time of my life!" he says. He's already planning to 11.... a huge party to celebrate when he returns. "It would be 12....fair not to share the fun!" he says.

Dylan has 13.... a deal with this newspaper, and he's agreed 14.... his first interview to our reporters after he lands back on 15....Earth!

0 a	saying	b	speaking	ⓒ	telling
1 a	im	b	un	c	dis
2 a	truth	b	true	c	honesty
3 a	un	b	im	c	in
4 a	telescope	b	spacecraft	c	asteroid
5 a	galaxy	b	comet	c	orbit
6 a	mentioned	b	offered	c	invited
7 a	warned	b	complained	c	explained
8 a	deep	b	heavy	c	strong
9 a	strange	b	ordinary	c	shallow
10 a	have	b	make	c	get
11 a	greet	b	throw	c	put
12 a	un	b	im	c	dis
13 a	given	b	put	c	made
14 a	us to give	b	to give	c	that he gives
15 a	planet	b	galaxy	c	solar

/ 15 points

Speaking

5 **Complete the conversation. Write one word in each blank.**

[Lily calls Oli.]

Lily Oli, I need your advice! I forgot to buy Adam a birthday present. Should I tell him?

Oli No! I ⁰ *wouldn't* tell him if I ¹ .... you, Lily. You know he'll be upset!

Lily Oh man … The fact is ² .... I've been really busy this week.

Oli Well, ³ .... don't you make him something?

Lily ⁴ .... way! I'm terrible at making things.

Oli Well, do you ⁵ .... you could make a chocolate cake? That isn't too difficult.

Lily That ⁶ .... sense. Thanks!

Oli I'll email you a good recipe. But make ⁷ .... you don't skip any of the instructions! And ⁸ .... careful not to burn the cake!

[Three hours later, Lily calls Oli again.]

Lily Oli, help! I burned the cake! You ⁹ .... to understand that I've never cooked before. I'm so sorry!

Oli OK, well, let's forget ¹⁰ .... it. I'm coming over. Maybe we can cook together.

Lily Thank you. You're amazing!

/ 10 points

Translation

6 **Translate the sentences.**

1 After he'd escaped from prison, he broke into a house.

....
....
....

2 They asked the astronaut to make a speech.

....
....
....

3 Who stayed up all night to look at the stars?

....
....
....

4 I warned her not to wear high heels, but she refused to listen.

....
....
....

5 They would have seen the comet if they hadn't been so impatient.

....
....
....

/ 5 points

Dictation

7 **Listen and write.**

31

1 ....
....
2 ....
....
3 ....
....
4 ....
....
5 ....
....

/ 5 points

Grammar Reference

• Will/Going to

will
He'll (will) help you. I won't (will not) help you.
Will you help me? Yes, we will./No, we won't.

going to
She's (is) going to work here. We aren't (are not) going to work here.
Are you going to work here? Yes, I am./No, I'm not.

Future time expressions

Tonight/Tomorrow, …
Next week/month/year …
This summer/weekend …
In a day/three days …
By Monday/the weekend/the end of the year …
In the next week/month/year …

Use

We use *will*:

- to express sudden decisions or thoughts made at the moment of speaking. These include offers, promises, requests and orders.
  A *I'm cold.*   **B** *I'll close the window.*
  Will you get here at nine tomorrow, please?

- to make or ask for a general prediction or guess about the future.
  Who do you think will get the job?
  I think he'll be famous one day.

We use *going to*:

- to talk about general plans or intentions for the future.
  I'm going to study art in college.
  He's going to speak to the manager tomorrow.

- to make predictions based on evidence at the moment of speaking.
  Look at those clouds. It's going to rain.
  Watch out! We're going to crash!

• Present simple and Present continuous for future

Present simple for future
The train leaves at 11:43 tomorrow. The next bus doesn't (does not) leave until lunchtime.
Does the concert start at eight? Yes, it does./No, it doesn't.

Present continuous for future
I'm (am) starting my new job next week. We aren't (are not) meeting them tonight.
Are you doing anything interesting this summer? Yes, we are./No, we aren't.

Use

- We use the Present simple to talk about scheduled events or timetables.
  The next train arrives in ten minutes.
  The stores close at five thirty.

- We use the Present continuous to talk about definite plans. We often mention a time or place.
  We're celebrating Sara's birthday this weekend.
  I'm meeting them outside the movie theater at eight o'clock.

- We do not use the Present simple to talk about plans.
  Ella is meeting us here tonight.
  NOT *Ella meets us here tonight.*

Grammar practice • Will/Going to

1 Match the uses (a–d) to the verbs in bold in the sentences (1–6).

a plan or intention
b spontaneous decision
c general prediction
d prediction based on evidence

1 I think you**'ll be** a very successful journalist.   c
2 We**'re going to study** German next year.
3 **A** These books are heavy.
   B I**'ll carry** them.
4 It's snowing. It**'s going to feel** cold today.
5 I probably **won't have** the same job all my life.
6 I**'m not going to eat** lunch in the office today.

2 Complete the future time expressions.

> by (x2)   in (x2)   ~~next~~   next

1 He's going to start a new job *next* week.
2 I'll call you .... two days.
3 We'll know the answer .... midday.
4 I'll finish the project sometime .... the next week.
5 We're going to move to a new house .... month.
6 I'm going to write the report .... the end of the day.

3 Choose the correct options.

1 **A** I lost my presentation!
   B Don't worry, I *'ll* / I'm going to help you.
2 He's coming this way! He *'ll* / *'s going to* walk right past us!
3 Have you decided what to do next? *Will you* / *Are you going to* text her?
4 **A** I'm really tired.
   B I *'ll* / *'m going to* get you a coffee.
5 **A** Do you have any plans for tonight?
   B Yes, I *'ll* / *'m going to* meet some friends.
6 I *won't* / *'m not going to* want to work here for more than a year.

4 Complete the sentences with *will* or *going to* and the verbs in parentheses.

1 She *'s going to leave* (leave) school next year.
2 Life .... (not stay) the same forever!
3 Be careful! You .... (drop) those cups!
4 **A** The phone's ringing.
   B I .... (answer) it.
5 We .... (not spend) this summer at home.
6 What .... (the world/be) like in 2050?

• Present simple and Present continuous for future

5 Choose the correct options.

Allie [1]*Do you take* / *Are you taking* a train into town tonight?

Ian Yes. Mom [2]*gives* / *is giving* me a ride to the station after dinner. The train [3]*leaves* / *is leaving* at 7:25.

Allie What time [4]*does it arrive* / *is it arriving*?

Ian At 7:50.

Allie But we [5]*meet* / *'re meeting* everyone at 8:00!

Ian I know, don't panic! The movie [6]*starts* / *is starting* at 8:15. There's plenty of time.

6 Write sentences with the Present simple or the Present continuous.

1 The office / open / at 8:30
   The office opens at 8:30.
2 Her plane / land / at midnight tonight
   ....
3 I / give / a presentation / here tomorrow
   ....
4 he / work / late / tonight / ?
   ....
5 The next bus / not stop / at the mall
   ....
6 We / not use the meeting room / after lunch
   ....

Grammar Reference

● Passive statements

Present simple	They repair the pier.	The pier is repaired.
Past simple	They repaired the pier.	The pier was repaired.
Future simple	They will repair the pier.	The pier will be repaired.

Use

We use the passive when we are more interested in talking about an action (the verb) than saying who or what does/did it (the agent).

*The seawall **will be rebuilt** next week.*
(Information about who will rebuild the seawall is unknown or not important.)

*The sandcastle **was washed** away by the waves.*
(We are particularly interested in the sandcastle and what happened to it.)

Form

● To form the passive, we use *(not)* be + past participle. We use *be* in the same tense that we would use in the active sentence.
*They **make** the ice cream here.* (Present simple active)
→ *The ice cream **is made** here.* (Present simple passive)

● When we change an active sentence into a passive sentence, the object of the active sentence becomes the subject of the passive sentence:

(object)
*They **restored** the beach chair.*

*The beach chair **was restored**.*
(subject)

By + agent

● If we want to include information about who or what does/did the action in a passive sentence, we use *by* + agent.

(subject)   (object)
*Gustave Eiffel **designed** the Eiffel Tower.*

*The Eiffel Tower **was designed** by Gustave Eiffel.*
(subject)   (agent)

● We include *by* + agent if the agent is important.
The Empire State Building was designed. ✗
(This sentence is incomplete!)
*The Empire State Building was designed **by William F. Lamb**.* ✓   (This is a complete sentence.)

● We omit *by* + agent if we do not know who or what the agent is, or if the agent is not important.
My bag was stolen.
NOT ~~My bag was stolen **by someone**.~~
The bridge will be painted.
NOT ~~The bridge will be painted **by some painters**.~~

● Passive questions

	Active	Passive
Present simple	Do they make it here?	Is it made here? Yes, it is./No, it isn't.
Past simple	Did they make it here?	Was it made here? Yes, it was./No, it wasn't.
Future simple	Will they make it here?	Will it be made here? Yes, it will./No, it won't.

Wh questions	
Active	**Passive**
Where do they sell them?	Where are they sold?
When did they build it?	When was it built?
What will they discover?	What will be discovered?

Form

● To form passive questions, we use the correct form of *be* + past participle: *Was it restored here?*

● If we need to include a subject in present and past passive questions, we put it after the verb *be*.
*Where **is the ice cream** made?*

● If we need to include a subject in future simple passive questions, we put it after *will* and before *be*.
*Where **will the seagulls be** released?*

● If we need to include *by* + agent, we add it to the end of the question.
*Was the photo taken **by your grandmother**?*

● If we want to ask who or what an agent is/was, we use *by* at the end of the question.
*Who was the photo taken **by**?*

Grammar practice

• Passive statements

1 **Write the tense:** *present*, *past* or *future*.
Then decide if the sentence is *active* or *passive*.

1 They **discovered** an island.
past   active

2 English **is spoken** here.

....

3 We**'ll visit** the coast.

....

4 The pier **wasn't repaired**.

....

5 The house **will be painted** soon.

....

6 Sorry, we **don't accept** pesos.

....

2 **Write the correct present, past or future passive form of the verbs.**

1 The new arcade *will be opened* (open)
next year.

2 The church .... (build)
in the eighteenth century.

3 The café .... (clean)
every night.

4 The beach .... (not/discover)
until 1540.

5 The wild birds ....
(not/release) tomorrow.

6 Sharks .... (not/see) here
very often these days.

3 **Rewrite the sentences in the passive. Begin the passive sentence with the noun in bold. Only include** *by* **+ agent where shown.**

1 Homer wrote **The Odyssey**.
The Odyssey was written by *Homer*.

2 People will film **the documentary** here.

....

3 Animal experts train **the dolphins**.

.... by ....

4 They organize **the event** every year.

....

5 Someone took **the photo** last year.

....

6 Wild animals won't eat **the food**.

.... by ....

4 **Cross out** *by* **+ agent when it isn't necessary.**

1 The fish are caught locally **by people**.

2 The town will be visited **by the president**.

3 My bag was stolen **by someone** yesterday.

4 This coast was painted **by Van Gogh**.

5 The house will be built **by builders** next year.

6 All the souvenirs are made **by local people**.

• Passive questions

5 **Make passive questions.**

1 made / the / sandcastles / How / are / ?
How are the sandcastles made?

2 born / were / you / Where / ?

....

3 held / Is / surfing contest / the / here / ?

....

4 treasure / Will / the / ever / discovered / be / ?

....

5 prizes / awarded / will / How / be / many / ?

....

6 the / earthquake / destroyed / Were / the /
buildings / in / ?

....

....

6 **Write passive questions. Use the tenses given.**

1 you / bite / ?   (past)
Were you bitten?

2 it / break / ?   (present)

....

3 When / it / invent / ?   (past)

....

4 the ship / save / ?   (future)

....

5 Where / the beach chairs / keep / ?   (present)

....

6 How long / the beach / close / ?   (future)

....

• First and Second conditional

First conditional

I'll (will) call you if I have time.
If they don't (do not) take a map, they won't (will not) find the island.
What will you do if it's (is) sunny tomorrow?

Second conditional

If I discovered a new star, I'd (would) be very happy.
He wouldn't travel into space if he didn't work for NASA.
If you had your own spacecraft, where would you go?

- Conditional sentences have two clauses: the conditional clause (starting with *if*) and the result clause.

  If I had a lot of money, | I'd travel around the word.
  (conditional clause) (result clause)

- We can use the clauses in any order, but we must use a comma when the conditional clause comes first.
  If I were you, I'd go. = I'd go if I were you.

First conditional

- We use the First conditional to talk about possible or probable future events or situations.
  I'll talk to her if she goes to the party.
  (She might go to the party. It's very likely.)

- We also use the First conditional to make promises and give warnings.
  I'll help you if you buy me a coffee.
  If you don't take a map, you'll get lost!

- To form the First conditional, we use
  if + Present simple, *will/won't* + infinitive.
  If you work harder, you'll improve.
  OR
  will/won't + infinitive + *if* + Present simple.
  You'll improve if you work harder.

Second conditional

- We use the Second conditional to talk about unlikely or impossible present or future events or situations.
  I'd buy a spacecraft if I became a billionaire.
  (I probably won't become a billionaire. It isn't very likely.)

- We also use the Second conditional to give advice.
  I'd tell them to be quiet if they were my children.

- To form the Second conditional, we usually use
  if + Past simple, *would(n't)* + infinitive.
  If he discovered a new island, he'd be very happy.
  OR
  would(n't) + infinitive + *if* + Past simple.
  He'd be very happy if he discovered a new island.

- The verb *to be* in the *if* clause of a Second conditional sentence most often takes the form *were* in American English.
  If he were taller, he would be a professional basketball player.
  If I were you, I would talk to the principal.

• Subject/Object questions

Subject questions

Which costs more?
Who discovered the island?

Object questions

How much does it cost?
What did he discover?

- When the question word is the object of a Present simple or Past simple question, we use *do/does/did*.

  How do you feel?
  (object) (subject)

  Who did he see?
  (object) (subject)

- When the question word is the subject of a Present simple or Past simple question, we do NOT use *do/does/did*.

  What happens now?
  (subject)

  Who saw you?
  (subject) (object)

Grammar practice • First and Second conditional

1 **Match the sentence beginnings (1–6) to the endings (a–f) to make sentences. Do the completed sentences include First (*1st*) or Second (*2nd*) conditional forms?**

1 If I were an astronaut,   ..f.. (2nd.)
2 If you look into the telescope, ... (.......)
3 If we see a comet tonight, ... (.......)
4 If the river weren't so wide, ... (.......)
5 If I didn't love adventure, ... (.......)
6 If it's cloudy at night, ... (.......)

a I'll be surprised.
b the stars won't shine as brightly.
c you'll see the planet Venus.
d we'd be able to cross it.
e I wouldn't be an explorer.
f I'd travel to Mars.

2 **Choose the correct options.**

1 If you wait here, I *'ll* / *'d* get the tickets.
2 If we had a map, we *'d* / *'ll* know where to go.
3 I'll go with you if you *like* / *liked*.
4 I *won't* / *wouldn't* be happy if they cancel the trip.
5 If I met an alien, I *won't* / *wouldn't* know what to do!
6 Where would you go if you *had* / *have* your own spacecraft?

3 **Are the situations (1–6) likely for these speakers? Fill in the blanks with the correct form of the verbs to make First or Second conditional sentences.**

1 **Your mom:** If I *were* (be) rich, I*'d travel* (travel) a lot.
2 **Famous singer:** If I .... (travel) a lot, I .... (meet) tons of fans.
3 **Astronaut:** I .... (keep) a video diary if I .... (go) into space.
4 **You:** If I .... (go) into space, I .... (look) for aliens!
5 **Your neighbor:** I .... (not know) what to do if I .... (see) a tiger.
6 **Nature moviemaker:** If we .... (not see) a tiger, we .... (be) disappointed.

Subject/Object questions

4 **Are these questions subject questions (*S*) or object questions (*O*)?**

1 Who helps you?   *S*
2 Who do you help?   ....
3 What moved?   ....
4 What did they move?   ....
5 How much does it weigh?   ....
6 Which weighs more?   ....

5 **Write subject and object questions. Add an auxiliary verb (*do/does/did*) if necessary.**

1 What kind of vacation / you / usually / ?   (prefer)
   What kind of vacation do you usually prefer?
2 What / last weekend / ?   (happen)
   ....
3 Who / he / yesterday / ?   (see)
   ....
4 Who / her / to dinner / last night / ?   (invite)
   ....
5 How fast / this spacecraft / ?   (fly)
   ....
6 How many / people / in your house / ?   (live)
   ....

6 **Write subject and object questions for the <u>underlined</u> information in the answers.**

1 *Which one looks better*?   (look)
   <u>The red one</u> looks better.
2 .... ?   (text)
   I texted <u>John</u>.
3 .... ?   (eat)
   We ate <u>hamburgers and hot dogs</u>.
4 .... ?   (give)
   <u>Mom</u> gives me the money.
5 .... ?   (happen)
   <u>Nothing</u> happened yesterday.
6 .... ?   (call)
   I call him <u>every week</u>.

Grammar Reference

• Past perfect

Affirmative		
I/He/She/It We/You/They	'd (had) escaped	by then.
Negative		
I/He/She/It We/You/They	hadn't (had not) escaped	by then.

Questions and short answers
Had I/he/she/it/we/you/they escaped **by then?**
Yes, I/he/she/it/we/you/they **had.**
No, I/he/she/it/we/you/they **hadn't.**

Wh questions
Where had you escaped **from?**

Irregular verbs have different past participle forms. (See the **Irregular Verb List**, Workbook page 141.)

Time expressions and sequencing words

after   already   before   by (+ a time)   by the time
for   just   since   when

*He'd **just** put on his disguise **when** the phone rang.*
***By the time** the rain stopped, everyone had **already** gone.*
*We'd known them **for many years**/**since we were in elementary school.***

Use

We use the Past perfect to talk about actions or situations that happened:

* before a specific moment in the past.
  ***By the time** he was twenty, he'd become a famous detective.*
  *I'd solved the problem **by eight o'clock.***

* before another action or situation in the past. We use the Past simple to talk about the later action or situation.
  *He'd left **before** I **arrived.** (He left. Then I arrived.)*
  *Before she **got** home, they'd **broken** into her house. (They broke into her house. Then she got home.)*

Form

We form the Past perfect with *had* + past participle.
She'd gone. I hadn't gone. Had they gone?

• Third conditional

Affirmative
If he'd (had) asked **me for help,** I'd (would) have helped **him.**
They'd (would) have escaped if she'd (had) given **them the key.**

Negative
If he hadn't (had not) followed **her,** he wouldn't (would not) have discovered **the truth.**
I wouldn't (would not) have been **angry with** you if **you** hadn't (had not) lied.

Questions
Would you have believed **me** if I'd (had) told **you the truth?**
If he'd (had) seen **the thief, what** would he have done?

Use

We use the Third conditional to talk about unreal situations or events in the past (situations or events that did not happen).

If they'd listened to me, they would have caught the spy.
(They didn't listen to me, so they didn't catch the spy.)
I wouldn't have screamed if I hadn't been scared.
(I was scared, so I screamed.)

Form

* To form the Third conditional, we use
  if + Past perfect, *would(n't) have* + past participle.
  *If he'd run, he **wouldn't have been** late.*
  OR
  would(n't) have + past participle + *if* + Past perfect.
  *He **wouldn't have been** late if he'd run.*

* We can use the conditional clause (starting with *if*) and the result clause in any order, but we must use a comma when the conditional clause comes first.
  If I'd known, I would have helped.
  I would have helped if I'd known.

Grammar practice • Past perfect

1. Complete the sentences with the Past perfect form of the verbs. Underline the action or event that happened first.

1 I arrived after the party *had ended* (end).
2 We left after the movie
.... (start).
3 Belle .... (eat) lunch before she went shopping.
4 By the time he was ten, Tom
.... (became) famous.
5 He .... (just/wake up) when the phone rang.
6 The robbery .... (already/happen) before we got home.

2. Choose the correct options.

1 They were late because they *stayed* / *'d stayed* too long at the café.
2 I*'d never seen* / *never saw* that woman before she appeared last night.
3 We *knew* / *'d known* each other for years before I learned the truth.
4 After we'd had lunch, we *drank* / *'d drunk* a coffee.
5 The concert still *didn't end* / *hadn't ended* by eleven o'clock.
6 **A** Had they put on their disguises before they *left* / *'d left*?
   B No, they *didn't* / *hadn't*.

3. Complete the sentences. Use a Past simple and a Past perfect form in each sentence.

1 She*'d studied* (study) French for years before she *moved* (move) to Paris.
2 After we .... (see) the menu, we .... (order) our meals.
3 They .... (just/sit) down when Max .... (appear).
4 By the time we .... (reach) the station, the train .... (already/leave).
5 I .... (want) to go to New York because I .... (never/be) there before.
6 I .... (not see) the movie before, so I .... (decide) to buy a ticket.

• Third conditional

4. Choose the correct options.

1 If I'd seen him, I would *have screamed* / *screamed*!
2 He would have caught the thief if he *ran* / *'d run* a little faster.
3 She would have reported him to the police if he *isn't* / *hadn't been* her brother.
4 If you'd locked the door, she *wouldn't get* / *wouldn't have gotten* in.
5 Would *you have stolen* / *have you stolen* the money if you'd found the wallet?
6 If he *didn't commit* / *hadn't committed* this crime, he wouldn't have gone to prison.

5. Complete the Third conditional sentences with the correct form of the verbs.

1 I*'d have passed* (pass) the law exam if I*'d worked* (work) harder.
2 He .... (escape) if he .... (not break) his leg.
3 If I .... (not become) a detective, I .... (be) a spy.
4 If you .... (call) the police, this .... (not happen).
5 What .... (you/do) if you .... (see) him?

6. Write Third conditional sentences about these situations.

1 He was poor, so he took the money.
   If he hadn't *been poor*, he *wouldn't have taken the money*.
2 They didn't follow us, so we were safe.
   If they'd .... ,
   we ....
3 She was in a hurry, so she didn't wait.
   If she hadn't .... ,
   she ....
4 I hid because I was scared.
   I wouldn't ....
   if I ....
5 We didn't see the movie because we didn't have enough money.
   We'd .... if we ....
6 I knew what to do after I'd read his message.
   I wouldn't ....
   if I ....

Grammar Reference

• Reported statements

Direct speech	Reported speech *I said/told her that …*
Present simple → "We dance."	**Past simple** … we danced.
Present continuous → "We're dancing."	**Past continuous** … we were dancing.
Past simple → "We danced."	**Past perfect** … we'd danced.
Present perfect → "We've danced."	**Past perfect** … we'd danced.
am/is/are going to → "We're going to dance."	***was/were going to*** … we were going to dance.
will/won't → "We'll dance."	***would/wouldn't*** … we would dance.
have to/must → "We have to dance." "We must dance."	***had to*** … we had to dance.
can → "We can dance."	***could*** … we could dance.

- When we report speech, we put the main verb one step back in time.
  "I broke it." → *He said that he'd broken it.*

- We do not use quotation marks in reported speech.

- We report statements with *said that* or *told* + indirect object + *that*.
  I said that it was OK. / I told her that it was OK.
  NOT *I said her that it was OK. / I told that it was OK.*

- We often need to change pronouns and possessive adjectives.
  "I lost my keys," she said. →
  She said that she'd lost her keys.

- We often change expressions of time and place.
  "I'll stay here tonight." →
  He said that he would stay there that night.

Direct speech → reported speech
now → then   today/tonight → that day/that night
this week → that week   yesterday → the day before
last month → the month before
five years ago → five years before
tomorrow → the next day
next year → the following year   here → there

• Reported commands and requests

Affirmative	
"Leave!" →	He told us to leave.
"Please leave." →	He asked us to leave.
Negative	
"Don't leave!" →	He told us not to leave.
"Please don't leave." →	He asked us not to leave.

- To report commands and requests, we use
  subject + *asked/told* + object (+ *not*) + infinitive.
  I told her not to shout.
  We asked them to stay.

- We don't use *please* in reported requests.

• Reported questions

Wh questions	
"Who is she?" →	I asked him who she was.
"When did it start?" →	She asked me when it had started.
Yes/No questions	
"Do you like me?" →	He asked me if I liked him.
"Will you help us?" →	They asked us if we'd help them.

- We do not use question marks (?) in reported questions.

- Tenses change, and pronouns, possessive adjectives and time and place expressions often change. See **Reported statements** (above).

- Reported questions keep the same word order as an affirmative sentence.
  "Where are you?" → *I asked her where she was.*
  NOT *I asked her where was she.*

- If a direct question uses question words (*who, what, how*, etc.), we repeat the same question words in the reported question.
  "How are you?" → *He asked me how I was.*

- If a direct question does NOT use question words (*who, what, how*, etc.), we use *if* in the reported question. We do not use *do/does/did*.
  "Do you know me?" → *She asked me if I knew her.*
  "Will you stay?" → *I asked her if she'd stay.*

Grammar practice • Reported statements

1 Write the correct reported speech form of the underlined verbs.

1 "I'm throwing a party!"
Dan told Ash that he *was throwing* a party.
2 "I decorated the house yesterday."
Dan said that he ....
the house the day before.
3 "I've emailed you an invitation."
Dan told Ash that he ....
her an invitation.
4 "I'll come!"
Ash said that she ....
5 "I can bring some music."
Ash told Dan that she ....
some music.
6 "The party is going to be great!"
Dan said that the party .... great.

2 Read the direct speech. Then complete the reported sentences with the correct pronouns, possessive adjectives and time and place expressions.

"¹ I had a great time at Olivia's party ² last night.
She invited a lot of people from ³ our school.
⁴ I'm meeting some of them ⁵ here later ⁶ today."

Nathan said that ¹ *he*'d had a great time at
Olivia's party ² .... He told Sophie
that Olivia had invited a lot of people from
³ .... school. He explained that
⁴ .... was meeting some of them
⁵ .... later ⁶ ....

3 Rewrite the sentences in reported speech.

1 Keira → Will: "We met a year ago."
Keira told *Will that they'd met the year before*.
2 I → them: "I really enjoyed your party."
I told ....
3 "I've never been here before."
I said ....
4 Vicki → me: "I'll call you next week."
Vicki told ....
5 "We must go now."
They said ....
6 Steve → Emma: "I love your dress."
Steve told ....

Reported commands and requests

4 Are these sentences commands (*C*) or requests (*R*)? Rewrite them in reported speech.

1 "Go away!"   .C.
2 "Please come in."   ....
3 "Stop talking!"   ....
4 "Please help."   ....
5 "Please don't go."   ....
6 "Don't sit there!"   ....

1 She *told* me *to go away*.
2 I .... them ....
3 The teacher ....
us ....
4 He .... me ....
5 I .... her ....
6 You .... him ....

Reported questions

5 Choose the correct options.

1 I asked her if *wanted she* / *she wanted* to come.
2 He asked me how *getting home I was* /
I was getting home.
3 They asked her who the guests *will be* /
would be.
4 She asked him *if* / *that* he could book a limo.
5 Mara asked you *did you like* / *if you liked*
the music.
6 Tim asked us how long *had we been* /
we'd been there.

6 Phil asks Layla a lot of questions at a party!
Rewrite his questions in reported speech.

1 "Do you want to dance?"
He asked her if she wanted to dance.
2 "Have we met before?"
....
3 "Can I get you a drink?"
....
4 "Did I tell you about my heavy metal band?"
....
5 "Do you want to meet tomorrow night?"
....
6 "Where are you going?"
....

Vocabulary

Work for It

Unit vocabulary

1 Translate the expressions.

Work collocations

answer the phone ....

attend a meeting ....

check emails ....

deal with inquiries ....

give a presentation ....

make an appointment

....

make some copies ....

order office supplies ....

prepare a spreadsheet

....

take payments ....

work at the front desk

....

write a report ....

2 Translate the words and phrases.

Job qualities

Adjectives

accurate ....

analytical ....

experienced ....

organized ....

patient ....

practical ....

punctual ....

reliable ....

Nouns and noun phrases

excellent IT skills ....

good communicator

....

leadership qualities ....

team player ....

Vocabulary extension

3 Match the objects in the picture to the words in the box. Use your dictionary if necessary. Write the words in English and in your language.

| bulletin board | copy machine | file(s) | keyboard | monitor | printer |

1 .... *file(s)* ....

2 ....

3 ....

4 ....

5 ....

6 ....

Vocabulary

Coast

Unit vocabulary

1 Translate the words.

Coastal life

arcade ....
beach chair ....
beach umbrella ....
cliffs ....
go-cart ....
harbor ....
hot dog stand ....
ice cream stand ....
pier ....
seagull ....
seawall ....
souvenir shop ....

2 Translate the words.

Verbs with prefixes *dis-* and *re-*

disagree ....
disappear ....
discontinue ....
discover ....
dislike ....
recover ....
release ....
remove ....
replace ....
research ....
restore ....

Vocabulary extension

3 Match the photos to the words in the box. Use your dictionary if necessary. Write the words in English and in your language.

| beach volleyball | fishing | kayaking |
| ~~sailing~~ | scuba diving | sunbathing |

1 .... *sailing* ....
....

2 ....
....

3 ....
....

4 ....
....

5 ....
....

6 ....
....

Final Frontiers

Unit vocabulary

1 Translate the words.

Adjective antonyms
ancient – modern
.... – ....
dark – light
.... – ....
deep – shallow
.... – ....
heavy – light
.... – ....
low – high
.... – ....
narrow – wide
.... – ....
ordinary – strange
.... – ....
temporary – permanent
.... – ....
weak – powerful/strong
.... – ..../
....

2 Translate the words.

Space	
asteroid	....
astronaut	....
astronomer	....
comet	....
galaxy	....
moon	....
orbit	....
planet	....
solar system	....
spacecraft	....
star	....
telescope	....

Vocabulary extension

3 Match the pictures to the pairs of adjective antonyms (e.g., *ancient/modern*) in the box. Use your dictionary if necessary. Write the words in English and in your language.

asleep	awake	dry	empty	full	~~wet~~

1 .... *wet* ....   2 ....
....

3 ....   4 ....
....

5 ....   6 ....
....

Vocabulary

Spies

 Translate the expressions.

Spy collocations

break into somewhere
....

decode a message
....

escape from somewhere
....

follow someone   ....

make a deal   ....

spy on someone   ....

take cover   ....

tap a phone   ....

tell a lie   ....

tell the truth   ....

track down a person
....

wear a disguise   ....

2 **Translate the words.**

Adjectives with prefixes *dis-*, *im-*, *in-*, *un-*

dishonest   ....

disloyal   ....

dissatisfied   ....

impatient   ....

impolite   ....

impossible   ....

inappropriate   ....

incorrect   ....

intolerant   ....

unfair   ....

unimportant   ....

unsuccessful   ....

3 **Match the pictures to the spy collocations in the box. Use your dictionary if necessary. Write the collocations in English and in your language.**

| do some research | ~~look for clues~~ | report a crime to the police |
| solve a crime | take notes | take photos |

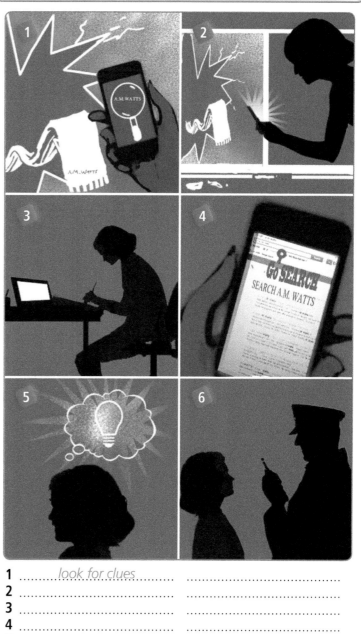

1 ....*look for clues*..........   ....
2 ....
3 ....
4 ....
5 ....
6 ....

Vocabulary 9

Celebrate!

Unit vocabulary

1 Translate the expressions.

Party collocations

do your hair ....

go by limo ....

greet your guests ....

have the time of your life

....

hire a DJ ....

make a speech ....

put up decorations ....

stay up all night ....

throw a party ....

wear a jacket and tie

....

wear casual clothes

....

wear dressy clothes ....

wear high heels ....

2 Translate the words.

Reporting verbs

verb + object (+ *not*) + infinitive

invite ....

warn ....

verb (+ *not*) + infinitive

agree ....

offer ....

promise ....

refuse ....

verb + *that* + reported statement

admit ....

complain ....

explain ....

mention ....

Vocabulary extension

3 Match the photos to the celebration and party collocations in the box. Use your dictionary if necessary. Write the collocations in English and in your language.

go to a wedding   have a barbecue   open presents
~~send invitations~~   set off fireworks   watch a parade

1 .... *send invitations* ....
....

2 ....
....

3 ....
....

4 ....
....

5 ....
....

6 ....
....

Speaking and Listening

Phone language

• Speaking

1 Complete the conversations. Write one word
44 in each blank. Then listen and check.

  1 **A** *My* name's Eloise Powell. I'd .... to speak to the manager, please.

    B I'll .... you to him. Just a moment.

  2 **A** Hello. I'm John Clarke. .... I speak to Mr. Sorvino, please?

    B I'll put him on now. Hold .... , please.

  3 **A** Hi. I'm Katie Matthews. I'm calling .... the cleaning job.

    B I'm sorry, the manager isn't here right now. Can I .... a message?

2 Complete the conversation with these phrases.
45 Then listen and check.

I'll transfer	I'll put	I'm calling about
~~my name's~~	I speak to	I take

Salesperson	Stu's Sports.
Maya	Hello. ¹ *My name's* Maya Smith. ² .... the weekend job that you advertised in *Sports Times*. Can ³ .... Elaine Flannigan, please?
Salesperson	⁴ .... her on now. Hold on, please. … I'm very sorry. Elaine isn't here, but you can speak to our assistant manager, Wayne. ⁵ .... you to him. Just a moment.
Wayne	Hi there, Wayne Hudson here. Can ⁶ .... a message? I'll pass it on to Elaine when she gets back.

• Listening

3 Listen to two phone conversations. Write *Lydia*,
46 *Steve*, *both* or *neither*.

Who

1 is calling the *May Art Gallery*?   *both*

2 wants to speak to Mrs. May?   ....

3 leaves a message with the receptionist?
  ....

4 is definitely going to an interview on Saturday?
  ....

5 just started a new job at the information desk?   ....

4 Listen again. Is the information below correct
46 (✓) or incorrect (✗)? Correct any mistakes.

Phone call A

1 Caller's first name: Lidia   ✗   *Lydia*

2 Caller's last name:
  Briteman   ....

3 Time of interview:
  10:45   ....

Phone call B

4 Time Mrs. May returns from lunch:
  1:30   ....

5 Caller's phone number:
  546–3979   ....

6 Time the gallery closes on Sunday:
  5:00   ....

Asking for and giving directions

• Speaking

1 Look at the maps and complete the conversations. Listen and check.

47

1 **A** Excuse me, could you tell me where the museum is?

B Go *past* the bookstore, and then turn

....

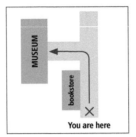

MUSEUM

bookstore

✕ You are here

2 **A** Excuse me, could you give me directions to the .... ?

B Take the .... turn on the right. You can't miss it!

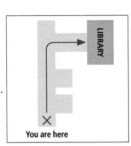

LIBRARY

✕ You are here

3 **A** Excuse me, how do I get to the station?

B Take the .... left. It's on the ....

STATION

✕ You are here

2 Choose the best options. Then listen and check.

48

Miguel ¹.... me, could you ².... me directions to the police station?

Woman Yes, of course. Turn right ³.... here. When you see the bank, ⁴.... the street. Go ⁵.... the drugstore, and then ⁶.... right. It's ⁷.... the left. You can't ⁸.... it.

1 a Sorry	**b** Afraid	**c** Excuse
2 a give	**b** send	**c** tell
3 a from	**b** to	**c** away
4 a take	**b** cross	**c** turn
5 a pass	**b** passed	**c** past
6 a take	**b** turn	**c** make
7 a at	**b** on	**c** about
8 a lose	**b** notice	**c** miss

• Listening

3 Listen to three conversations. Which places are mentioned?

49

1 hot dog stand ✓
2 aquarium
3 post office
4 seawall
5 church
6 harbor
7 ice cream stand
8 bank
9 souvenir shop
10 beach
11 art gallery
12 pier

4 Listen again and complete the table.

49

How long is the journey?		
Journey 1	¹ ten minutes	
Journey 2	² .... minutes	
Journey 3	³ .... minutes	
What should the visitors do?		
Journey 1	Order ⁴ .... with hot dog.	
Journey 2	Watch the ⁵ .... feeding.	
Journey 3	Take photos of the colorful ⁶	

Giving warnings

• Speaking

1 Match the sentences (1–5) to the replies (a–e) to complete the conversations. Then listen and check.

1 We're going up the mountain. *e*
2 I'm going to try to jump across the river.
3 We're going to pick mushrooms.
4 I'm going to put up my tent here.
5 I'm going to apologize.

a Watch out for the poisonous ones!
b Be careful not to fall in!
c OK. But be careful not to upset her!
d I wouldn't camp on the beach if I were you.
e Watch out for falling rocks!

2 Complete the conversation. Write one or two words in each blank. Then listen and check.

Joy   I'm going to my first music festival next weekend! Any advice?

Ali   Make ¹ *sure* you're not late.

Leah   Yes, and be careful ² .... lose your ticket! You're *so* forgetful.

Zoe   Watch ³ .... thieves! I wouldn't take too much money if ⁴ .... you.

Xavier   Oh, and ⁵ .... sure you ⁶ .... forget to text us!

• Listening

3 Listen to the conversation. Match the locations (1–6) to the items (a–f).

1 in the closet   *f*
2 on the chair   ....
3 in a drawer   ....
4 on a small table   ....
5 under the bed   ....
6 on the desk   ....

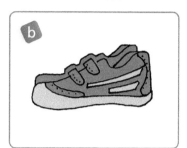

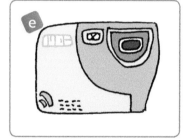

4 Listen again. Answer the questions.

1 Who is talking?
   Freya and her mom
2 Why is her mom annoyed?
   Freya hasn't finished .... for her trip.
3 What kind of trip is Freya going on?
   A ....
4 What does she want to borrow?
   A ....
5 What *doesn't* Freya's mom think she should take?
   A ....
6 Why?
   She thinks it's ...., and Freya .... it.

Speaking and Listening

Explaining and apologizing

● Speaking

1 **Choose the best options. Then listen and check.**
53

Dora Liam! I'm really angry with you. ¹.... did you take my bike?

Liam Oh man. The ².... is that I was late for work at the gym. If I'm late, I might lose my job!

Dora I'm ³.... of that. But you should ask!

Liam I know ⁴.... . You have to ⁵.... that I was in a hurry, and I couldn't find you. I did try!

Dora Oh, I'm sure that's ⁶.... .

Liam Dora, I'm sorry ⁷.... I took your bike. I won't do it again, I promise.

Dora Oh, let's ⁸.... about it. It's kind of funny anyway. I bet everyone at work laughed when they saw you riding a pink bike!

1 **a** How	**(b)** Why	**c** What
2 **a** fact	**b** story	**c** reality
3 **a** awake	**b** knowing	**c** aware
4 **a** this	**b** that	**c** it
5 **a** see	**b** know	**c** understand
6 **a** true	**b** so	**c** certain
7 **a** about	**b** that	**c** for
8 **a** lose	**b** stop	**c** forget

2 **Complete the conversations. Write one or two**
54 **words in each blank. Then listen and check.**

1 **A** I'm so ¹*sorry* that I upset you. I didn't realize that you were scared of spiders!

B Oh, I'm sure ².......................... true. I know it was just a joke. ³.......................... forget about it, OK?

2 **A** Why won't you let me go to the party?! The fact ⁴.......................... you don't trust me.

B No, that's not true. But ⁵.......................... to understand that we're your parents, so …

A I'm aware ⁶.......................... !

B I hadn't finished! We're your parents, so we worry about you.

● Listening

3 **Listen to the conversation. Then answer**
55 **the questions. Write C (*Chloe*) or J (*Jason*).**

Who
1 expresses anger?   *J*
2 explains why he/she did something bad?   ....
3 is worried about something?   ....
4 apologizes?   ....
5 offers help?   ....
6 extends an invitation?   ....

4 **Listen again. Are the statements true (T),**
55 **false (F) or don't know (DK)?**

1 When Jason arrives, Chloe is looking at his books.   *T*
2 Chloe is copying Jason's French homework.   ....
3 Chloe is worried about chemistry.   ....
4 Chloe failed most of her exams last time.   ....
5 Jason never asks for help with school subjects.   ....
6 Chloe and Jason are meeting on the weekend.   ....
7 Chloe usually wins computer games.   ....

Speaking and Listening

Reaching an agreement

• Speaking

1 Put the words in the correct order. Then listen
56 and check.

1 **A** *I think we should go home.*
go / home / I / should / think / we
B No way! The party's just getting started!

2 **A** ....
don't / Why / walk / we / there / ?
B That makes sense.

3 **A** ....
can / Maybe / make / we / decorations /
some
B I agree. I think we should have a Halloween
theme!

4 **A** ....
stay / Do / think / you / with Ava / we /
could / ?
B ....
good / a / idea / That's
I'll ask her.

2 Complete the conversation with these words and
57 phrases. Then listen and check.

a good idea	could	don't we	~~maybe~~
sense	should	think	way

Mary How are we going to get to the festival?
¹ *Maybe* we can take a train.

Ethan That's ² .... , but it's a really
long walk from the station. Do you think
your brother ³ .... give us
a ride?

Mary I don't think we ⁴ ....
ask him! He's a terrible driver.
Why ⁵ .... take a taxi?

Ethan No ⁶ .... ! A taxi would be
really expensive. I ⁷ .... we
should take a bus and save our money
for food, drinks and band T-shirts.

Mary That makes ⁸ ....
Let's do that!

• Listening

3 Listen to the conversation. Number the activities
58 in the order you hear them.

4 Listen again. Choose the correct options.
58
1 When is Ellie's birthday?
a the 10th **b** the 16th **c** the 21st
2 What *didn't* happen to Ellie this month?
a Her dog died.
b She failed her science test.
c She lost a singing contest.
3 Who likes karaoke?
a Kev **b** Ashley **c** Blake
4 What kind of movie *doesn't* Ellie like?
a comedy **b** fantasy **c** horror
5 Who works at the pizza place?
a a friend from school
b Blake
c someone in Blake's family

Pronunciation

Consonants

Symbol	Example	Your examples
/p/	pen	
/b/	book	
/t/	tea	
/d/	desk	
/k/	cat	
/g/	girl	
/tʃ/	cheese	
/dʒ/	June	
/f/	five	
/v/	very	
/θ/	thin	
/ð/	then	
/s/	so	
/z/	zoo	
/ʃ/	she	
/ʒ/	usually	
/h/	hat	
/m/	man	
/n/	now	
/ŋ/	thing	
/l/	long	
/r/	red	
/y/	yes	
/w/	week	

Vowels

Symbol	Example	Your examples
/ɪ/	sit	
/ɛ/	ten	
/æ/	black	
/ɑ/	hot	
/ʌ/	up	
/ʊ/	full	
/i/	see	
/eɪ/	pay	
/aɪ/	why	
/ɔɪ/	enjoy	
/u/	too	
/ou/	home	
/aʊ/	loud	
/ɪr/	year	
/ɛr/	wear	
/ɑr/	far	
/ɔ/	dog	
/ʊr/	sure	
/ɔr/	door	
/ə/	ago	
/ɚ/	shirt	

Pronunciation practice

Unit 1 • Compound noun word stress

1 Listen and repeat. Then mark the main stress
59 in each word. Answer the question below.

1 classmate   4 spaceship
2 lighthouse   5 snowmobile
3 skyscraper   6 windmill

Do we usually stress the *first*, *second* or *last*
syllable in compound nouns?   ....

2 Mark the main stress. Then listen, check
60 your answers and repeat.

1 bedroom   4 hairstylist
2 whiteboard   5 supermarket
3 notebook   6 newspaper

Unit 2 • Sentence stress

1 Listen and repeat. Then mark the stressed words.
61
1 We're happy because we made it to the finals.
2 Can you help me? Do these clothes
   go together?
3 You've made our dreams come true.

> **Brain Trainer**
>
> **Sentence stress**
> We usually stress the most important content words in
> sentences (often main verbs, nouns and adjectives).
>
> **Now do Exercise 2.**

2 Mark the *three* most important content words in
62 each sentence. Then listen, check your answers
and repeat the sentences, copying the stress.

1 I've made a very big decision.
2 My sister has moved to Alaska.
3 We went for a walk in the park.
4 Have you heard the news? I'm so excited!

Unit 3 • Showing feelings

1 Listen. You will hear a speaker say "Did you
63 see that?" in four different conversations.
Is the speaker *afraid*, *angry*, *bored* or *excited*?

1 ....   3 ....
2 ....   4 ....

2 Read the sentences. Do you think the speakers will
64 sound *afraid*, *angry*, *bored* or *excited*? Listen, check
your answers and repeat, copying the intonation.

1 I won the lottery!
2 There's nothing to do here.
3 What's that noise?
4 Never lie to me again!

Unit 4 • Consonant clusters

1 Listen and repeat. Do the <u>underlined</u> letters
65 have *one*, *two* or *three* consonant sounds?

a <u>squ</u>are   hel<u>ps</u>   e<u>x</u>pensive
b wea<u>th</u>er   <u>wh</u>ite   si<u>ck</u>
c buil<u>d</u>ing   ti<u>met</u>able   fini<u>sh</u>ed

2 <u>Underline</u> the consonant clusters. Then listen
66 and repeat.

1 The bus stops on a quiet street.
2 I remember her wonderful home in the country.
3 He found her passport in the suitcase.

Unit 5 • /ɚ/ and /ɔr/

1 Listen and repeat. Then <u>underline</u> the sounds
67 /ɚ/ or /ɔr/.

/ɚ/   learn   third   dessert
/ɔr/ warm   before   north

2 Complete the table. Then listen, check and repeat.
68

aff<u>or</u>d   b<u>or</u>ed   <u>ear</u>ly   fl<u>oor</u>   j<u>our</u>ney   w<u>or</u>ld

/ɚ/	/ɔr/
....	....
....	....
....	....

Unit 6 • Weak vs strong form of *was*

(1) **Listen and repeat, paying attention to**
69 **the strong and weak forms of *was*.**
Then answer the question below.

1 **A** Are you cold?
   B I **was** (/wɑz/), but I'm warmer now.
      It **was** (/wəz/) freezing earlier!

2 **A Was** (/wəz/) the pier closed yesterday?
   B Yes, it **was** (/wɑz/).

Do we say /wɑz/ or /wəz/ when we want
to emphasize **was**?   ....

(2) **Do you think the speaker will use strong (*S*) or**
70 **weak (*W*) forms of the words in bold? Listen,**
check your answers and repeat.

A The beach party ¹**was** (.....) amazing.
B ²**Was** (.....) Bart there?
A Yes, he ³**was** (.....)!
   He ⁴**was** (.....) the DJ.
B Really? Wow! He **was** (.....) awfully shy
   a few years ago.
A Yes, he ⁶**was** (.....) shy before. But he
   isn't now!

Unit 7 • Elided syllables

(1) **Listen and repeat. Write the number of syllables**
71 **you hear (1, 2, 3). Then cross out the silent**
syllables (the letters that you *don't* hear).

1 listening   ....
2 average   ....
3 memory   ....
4 musically   ....

(2) **Cross out the silent syllables in the words in bold.**
72 **Then listen, check your answers and repeat.**

1 He worked for **several businesses**,
   but the work made him **miserable**.
2 My main **interests** are **literature** and
   photography. I have three **cameras**!
3 **Every evening** we went to a **different**
   restaurant.

Unit 8 • /ɛr/ and /eɪ/

(1) **Listen and repeat. Match the headings (a–c)**
73 **to the columns (1–3) in the table.**

a /ɛr/ (w**ear**)   b /i/ (d**ea**l)   c /eɪ/ (br**ea**k)

1	2	3 ....
t**ea**m	gr**ea**t	b**ear**
s**ea**t	st**ea**k	p**ear**

(2) **Which word does *not* include the sound?**
74 **Listen and check your answers.**

1 /ɛr/ squ**are** st**air** st**ay**
2 /i/   b**ea**ch   p**eo**ple   p**air**
3 /eɪ/ m**ai**n   m**e**ter   mist**ake**
4 /ɛr/ **age**   **air**port   anywh**ere**
5 /i/   sc**a**red   s**e**cret   sp**ea**k
6 /eɪ/ w**ai**ter   w**ea**k   w**ei**ght

Unit 9 • /ʃ/, /ʒ/ and /dʒ/

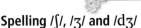

Brain Trainer

Spelling /ʃ/, /ʒ/ and /dʒ/
We can spell the sounds /ʃ/, /ʒ/ and /dʒ/ in different
ways. For example, we can write /ʃ/ as *sh* (*show*),
s (*sure*), *ci* (*delicious*) and *ti* (*pronunciation*).

Now do Exercises 1 and 2.

(1) **Listen and repeat. Write the missing letters**
75 **to complete the words.**

/ʃ/	/ʒ/	/dʒ/
wa**sh**	A**s**ia	fri**dge**
¹.....ugar	³u.....ually	⁵.....uice
²spe.....al	⁴deci.....on	⁶langua.....

(2) **Match the words in bold (1–6) to the sounds**
76 **(a–c). Then listen and check your answers.**

a /ʃ/   b /ʒ/   c /dʒ/

A I ¹**should** (.....) make some ²**introductions**
   (.....) … Nellie, this is Martin.
B It's a ³**pleasure** (.....) to meet you, Martin. I like
   your ⁴**jacket** (.....)! It's ⁵**unusual** (.....).
C Thanks! Listen, Nellie, this might sound
   ⁶**strange** (.....), but haven't we met before?

Irregular Verb List

Verb	Past Simple	Past Participle
be	was/were	been
become	became	become
begin	began	begun
break	broke	broken
bring	brought	brought
build	built	built
buy	bought	bought
can	could	been able
catch	caught	caught
choose	chose	chosen
come	came	come
cost	cost	cost
cut	cut	cut
do	did	done
draw	drew	drawn
drink	drank	drunk
drive	drove	driven
eat	ate	eaten
fall	fell	fallen
feed	fed	fed
feel	felt	felt
fight	fought	fought
find	found	found
fly	flew	flown
forget	forgot	forgotten
get	got	gotten
give	gave	given
go	went	gone/been
have	had	had
hear	heard	heard
hold	held	held
keep	kept	kept
know	knew	known
leave	left	left
lend	lent	lent

Verb	Past Simple	Past Participle
light	lit	lit
lose	lost	lost
make	made	made
mean	meant	meant
meet	met	met
pay	paid	paid
put	put	put
read /rid/	read /rɛd/	read /rɛd/
ride	rode	ridden
ring	rang	rung
run	ran	run
say	said	said
see	saw	seen
sell	sold	sold
send	sent	sent
shine	shone	shone
show	showed	shown
sing	sang	sung
sit	sat	sat
sleep	slept	slept
speak	spoke	spoken
spend	spent	spent
stand	stood	stood
steal	stole	stolen
swim	swam	swum
take	took	taken
teach	taught	taught
tell	told	told
think	thought	thought
throw	threw	thrown
understand	understood	understood
wake	woke	woken
wear	wore	worn
win	won	won
write	wrote	written

My Assessment Profile Unit

1 **What can I do? Mark (✓) the options in the table.**

◄◄ = I need to study this again.   ❙❙ = I'm not sure about this.   ▶ = I'm happy with this.   ▶▶ = I do this very well.

		◄◄	❙❙	▶	▶▶
Vocabulary (pages 4 and 7)	• I can use verb and noun collocations to talk about things we might see, use or do at work. • I can use adjectives and phrases to describe people's personal job qualities.				
Pronunciation (page 4)	• I can recognize and pronounce words with the sounds /ɚ/ and /ɔr/ correctly.				
Reading (pages 5 and 10)	• I can read and understand a webpage about work experience and an article about jobs of the future.				
Grammar (pages 6 and 9)	• I can use *will* or *going to* correctly to talk about the future. • I can use a variety of future time phrases. • I can understand when to use the Present simple or the Present continuous to talk about the future.				
Speaking (pages 8 and 9)	• I can make a phone call. • I can leave and take a phone message.				
Listening (pages 8–10)	• I can understand a phone conversation and a conversation between friends.				
Writing (page 11)	• I can express degrees of certainty. • I can write an email about future plans.				

2 **What new words and expressions can I remember?**

words ....

expressions ....

3 **How can I practice other new words and expressions?**

record them on my MP3 player ☐   write them in a notebook ☐

practice them with a friend ☐   translate them into my language ☐

4 **What English have I learned outside class?**

	words	expressions
on the radio		
in songs		
in movies		
on the Internet		
on TV		
with friends		

My Assessment Profile Unit

1 **What can I do? Mark (✓) the options in the table.**

⏪ = I need to study this again.   ⏸ = I'm not sure about this.   ▶ = I'm happy with this.   ⏩ = I do this very well.

		⏪	⏸	▶	⏩
Vocabulary (pages 14 and 17)	• I can use twelve nouns to talk about things we might see at the coast. • I can use eleven verbs with the prefixes *dis-* and *re-*.				
Reading (pages 15 and 20)	• I can read and understand two descriptions of seaside towns and an article about a famous pirate.				
Grammar (pages 16 and 19)	• I can use the present, past and future passive. • I can use the passive with *by* + agent. • I can use the passive in questions.				
Pronunciation (page 16)	• I can understand when to use *was* with a weak or strong pronunciation.				
Speaking (pages 18 and 19)	• I can ask for and give directions.				
Listening (pages 18–20)	• I can understand someone giving directions and a tour guide giving information.				
Writing (page 21)	• I can use paragraphs or sections to organize my ideas clearly. • I can write a field trip report.				

2 **What new words and expressions can I remember?**

words ....

expressions ....

3 **How can I practice other new words and expressions?**

record them on my MP3 player ☐   write them in a notebook ☐
practice them with a friend ☐   translate them into my language ☐

4 **What English have I learned outside class?**

	words	expressions
on the radio		
in songs		
in movies		
on the Internet		
on TV		
with friends		

My Assessment Profile Unit

1 **What can I do? Mark (✓) the options in the table.**

⏪ = I need to study this again.   ⏸ = I'm not sure about this.   ▶ = I'm happy with this.   ⏩ = I do this very well.

		⏪	⏸	▶	⏩
Vocabulary (pages 28 and 31)	• I can use adjective antonyms to express opposite meanings. • I can use twelve nouns to talk about space.				
Pronunciation (page 28)	• I can pronounce words with elided syllables correctly.				
Reading (pages 29 and 34)	• I can read and understand an article about places to explore on Earth and an interview about a space colony.				
Grammar (pages 30 and 33)	• I can use all forms of the First and Second conditional. • I can understand when to use the First conditional or the Second conditional. • I can use subject and object questions correctly.				
Speaking (pages 32 and 33)	• I can give warnings.				
Listening (pages 32–34)	• I can understand a conversation between friends and three different people talking about space colonies.				
Writing (page 35)	• I can use the correct layout and expressions in a formal letter. • I can write an application letter.				

2 **What new words and expressions can I remember?**

words   ....

expressions   ....

3 **How can I practice other new words and expressions?**

record them on my MP3 player   ☐   write them in a notebook   ☐
practice them with a friend   ☐   translate them into my language   ☐

4 **What English have I learned outside class?**

	words	expressions
on the radio		
in songs		
in movies		
on the Internet		
on TV		
with friends		

My Assessment Profile Unit

1 **What can I do? Mark (✓) the options in the table.**

⏪ = I need to study this again.   ⏸ = I'm not sure about this.   ▶ = I'm happy with this.   ⏩ = I do this very well.

		⏪	⏸	▶	⏩
Vocabulary (pages 38 and 41)	• I can use twelve collocations to talk about spying. • I can form adjectives with the prefixes *dis-, im-, in-* and *un-*.				
Pronunciation (page 38)	• I can recognize and pronounce words with the sounds /ɛr/, /i/ and /eɪ/ correctly.				
Reading (pages 39 and 44)	• I can read and understand an extract from a spy novel and an article about surveillance in schools.				
Grammar (pages 40 and 43)	• I can use all forms of the Past perfect. • I can understand when to use the Past perfect or the Past simple. • I can use all forms of the Third conditional.				
Speaking (pages 42 and 43)	• I can apologize and explain why I did something. • I can acknowledge someone else's explanation.				
Listening (pages 42–44)	• I can understand conversations between friends and family members and a report.				
Writing (page 45)	• I can organize my ideas into clear paragraphs. • I can use different expressions to give opinions, introduce points and conclude. • I can write an opinion essay.				

2 **What new words and expressions can I remember?**

words ....

expressions ....

3 **How can I practice other new words and expressions?**

record them on my MP3 player ☐   write them in a notebook ☐

practice them with a friend ☐   translate them into my language ☐

4 **What English have I learned outside class?**

	words	expressions
on the radio		
in songs		
in movies		
on the Internet		
on TV		
with friends		

My Assessment Profile Unit

1 **What can I do? Mark (✓) the options in the table.**

◀◀ = I need to study this again. ❚❚ = I'm not sure about this. ▶ = I'm happy with this. ▶▶ = I do this very well.

		◀◀	❚❚	▶	▶▶
Vocabulary (pages 48 and 51)	• I can use thirteen collocations to talk about parties. • I can use ten reporting verbs with the correct reported speech structures.				
Pronunciation (page 48)	• I can recognize and pronounce words with the sounds /ʃ/, /ʒ/ and /dʒ/ correctly.				
Reading (pages 49 and 54)	• I can read and understand an article about proms and an article about different coming-of-age ceremonies.				
Grammar (pages 50, 51 and 53)	• I can report affirmative and negative statements in different tenses using *said* and *told*. • I can report affirmative and negative commands and requests. • I can report questions.				
Speaking (pages 52 and 53)	• I can make suggestions. • I can agree and disagree with suggestions.				
Listening (pages 52–54)	• I can understand a conversation between friends and a radio interview.				
Writing (page 55)	• I can use pronouns and possessive adjectives to avoid repeating ideas. • I can write a letter giving advice.				

2 **What new words and expressions can I remember?**

words ....
expressions ....

3 **How can I practice other new words and expressions?**

record them on my MP3 player ☐   write them in a notebook ☐
practice them with a friend ☐   translate them into my language ☐

4 **What English have I learned outside class?**

	words	expressions
on the radio		
in songs		
in movies		
on the Internet		
on TV		
with friends		

Notes

Notes

Notes

Notes

Notes

Pearson Education Limited
Edinburgh Gate
Harlow
Essex CM20 2JE
England
and Associated Companies throughout the world.

www.pearsonelt.com/moveit

© Pearson Education Limited 2015

The right of Katherine Stannett, Fiona Beddall and Bess Bradfield to be identified as the authors of this work has been asserted by them in accordance with the Copyright, Designs and Patents Act, 1988.

First published 2015
Fifth impression 2019
Set in 10.5/12.5pt LTC Helvetica Neue Light
ISBN: 978-1-2921-0138-5
Printed and bound by CPI Group (UK) Ltd, Croydon, CR0 4YY

Acknowledgements

We are grateful to the following for permission to reproduce copyright material:
Article 1.3 adapted from www.hackneygazette.co.uk/news/bee_inspired_how_bee_keeping_changed_one_man's_life_1_101162, Hackney Gazette; Emma Bartholomew; September 2011

Photo Acknowledgements

The publisher would like to thank the following for their kind permission to reproduce their photographs:

(Key: b-bottom; c-centre; l-left; r-right; t-top)

Students' Book:
Alamy Images: Bob Daemmrich Photography / Marjorie Kamys Cotera 44cl, epa european pressphoto agency b.v. 69tr, Mary Evans Picture Library 69bl, eye35.pix 14/2, Mim Friday 16tr, Gary Hebding Jr. 69br, Classic Image 57, Images of Africa Photobank 15/4, Justin Kase z15z 28/2, Loop Images Ltd 14/3, Mark Richardson 48 (b), Wild Places Photography / Chris Howes 29tl; **BNPS:** 16bl; **Bridgeman Art Library Ltd:** Peter Newark Historical Pictures / Private Collection / English School, (20th century) / Blackbeard (colour litho) 20bl; **Corbis:** Stan Fellerman 47r, JAI / Nadia Isakova 14/6, Charles & Josette Lenars 37b, Mika 5r, Ocean 49b, Reuters / Lucy Pemoni 70bl, Sygma / Herve Collart 54 (a), ZUMA Press / Ruaridh Stewart 28/1; **Fotolia.com:** Franny-Anne 14/12; **Getty Images:** AFP 23tl, Britain on View / Martin Leigh 14/9, Winston Davidian 44br, Digital Vision / Andrew Bret Wallis 68br, The Image Bank / DreamPictures 5l, Minden Pictures / Matthias Breiter 28/5, Photodisc / Steve Allen 50, Photographer's Choice / Ron Levine 48 (c), Photographer's Choice / Zac Macaulay 29r, Stone / Javier Pierini 10cl, The Image Bank / Daisy Gilardini 30, Universal Images Group / Eco Images 29bl, Ian Waldie 44tr; **innocent ltd:** 13tl, 13r; **iStockphoto:** oblachko 23tr, 47tr; **Rich Matheson:** 54 (d); **Pearson Education Ltd:** Gareth Boden 8, 18, 32, 42, 52; **Photolibrary.com:** Brand X Pictures / Verity Jane Smith 49t; **Press Association Images:** AP / Evert-Jan Daniels 23br, AP / Robert Willett 20tr, AP / Stephan Kogelman 23c; **Rex Features:** 10tr, 19, Nils Jorgensen 65, Quirky China News 28/3, Sinopix 54 (c); **Robert Harding World Imagery:** John Miller 14/8; **Science Photo Library Ltd:** British Antarctic Survey 28/6, NASA 37tl; **Shutterstock.com:** Alexey VI B 62, Helga Esteb 48 (d), F29 14l, David Hughes 14/10, Inc 15/2, jiawangkun 18c, Kzenon 14/1, Losevsky Photo and Video 42 (Laptop screen boy 2), Lissandra Melo 15/3, Menna 44tl, Monkey Business Images 42 (Laptop screen boy 1), 42 (Laptop screen girl 1), okili77 15 (A), PHB.cz (Richard Semik) 14/5, PhotoSky 15/1, Tomislav Pinter 47l, Poznyakov 68tr, Sorbis 42 (Laptop screen girl 2), Swellphotography 14/7, TachePhoto 14/4; **Sozaijiten:** 28/4; **SuperStock:** age fotostock / Grant Rooney 70tl, age fotostock / Ian Murray 21, Blend Images 54 (b), Fancy Collection 15 (boy), 15 (girl), image100 68bl, Gerard Lacz Images 10cr, Loop Images / Chris Warren 14/11, National Geographic 70tr, SuperFusion / Pressmaster 48 (a)

Workbook:
Alamy Images: Dygiclick 129tr, Gary Roebuck 132cr; **Corbis:** Macduff Everton 91bl, Lauryn Ishak 91tl, Gideon Mendel 132br; **Fotolia.com:** 142-146; **Getty Images:** Flickr 132cl, Stone / Britt Erlanson 132bl; **Pearson Education Ltd:** Steve Shott 80tr; **PhotoDisc:** 116; **Rex Features:** Everett Collection 101, Ray Tang 80cl; **Shutterstock.com:** American Spirit 89, chrisdorney 91cl, Dariush M 129br, R. Gino Santa Maria 114b, JeniFoto 81r, JonMilnes 129cr, Mictoon 132tl, Olegusk 95, Pressmaster 129bl, stocknadia 114t, TTphoto 129tl, ValeStock 81l; **SuperStock:** Blend Images 114, Corbis 85tr, Cultura Limited 132tr, Flirt 80br, Image Source 110, 129cl, Westend61 94, Yuri Arcurs Media 107

Cover images: *Front:* **Corbis:** PhotoAlto / Laurence Mouton

All other images © Pearson Education

Every effort has been made to trace the copyright holders and we apologise in advance for any unintentional omissions. We would be pleased to insert the appropriate acknowledgement in any subsequent edition of this publication.

Special thanks to the following for their help during location photography: East Herts District Council; Harlow Town Council; Naze Tower www.nazetower.co.uk; Tendring Council; Matthew Dickin; Jackie Dynamou; Anne and Ben Meaden; JoJo Notley

Illustrated by

Students' Book:
Peskimo; Paula Franco; Moreno Chiacchiera; Chris Coady; Matt Roussel.

Workbook:
Chris Coady; Julian Mosedale; Paula Franco; Peskimo.